Direct Analysis

Selected Papers

Direct Analysis

========== *Selected Papers*

By

JOHN N. ROSEN, M.D.

Grune & Stratton

New York   1953

Acknowledgments

Paper 1 was prepared originally for this book, Nov., 1952.

Paper 2 was published in *The Psychiatric Quarterly*, vol. 20, pp. 183–198, April, 1946.

Paper 3 was published originally in *The Psychiatric Quarterly*, vol. 21, pp. 117–119, Jan., 1947; addendum written for this book.

Paper 4 is a revised version based on a paper entitled "Some Etiological Concepts with a Verbatim Case Report on the Application of the Direct Analytical Method," read before the Washington Psychoanalytic Group, Nov. 8, 1947; the Schilder Society, Nov. 19, 1947; The Baltimore City Medical Society, Nov. 20, 1947; The Winter and Menninger Professional Personnel, Jan. 19, 1948; The Massachusetts Psychiatric Society, Mar. 11, 1948.

Paper 5 is a revised version of an article published originally in the *Bulletin of the Menninger Clinic,* vol. 14, No. 3, May, 1950.

Paper 6 is a revised version based on a paper entitled "The Optimum Conditions for the Treatment of Schizophrenic Psychosis by Direct Analytic Therapy," read before the New York Psychoanalytic Society, June 13, 1950.

Paper 7 is based on two informal lectures, one at Worcester State Hospital, Worcester, Massachusetts, Jan. 19, 1951; the other at The Veterans Administration Hospital, Northampton, Massachusetts, Oct. 23, 1951.

Paper 8 is a transcript of an interview conducted before the professional staff on the Veterans Administration Hospital, Northampton, Massachusetts, Oct. 23, 1951.

Paper 9 was published originally in *The Psychoanalytic Quarterly,* vol. 21, No. 3, 1952; minor revisions made and a new addendum written for this book.

To My Wife

Preface

THE PATIENT'S MOUTH is pulled and distorted as with pain. As sick as his mind is, he has still not lost the faculty of expressing his thoughts with speech. He says it isn't a pain; he says it's an ache. He has been going to the dentist with it, pain or ache, for 15 years but to no avail. He has been to the hospital and has had many shock treatments, but still he has that awful torture in his mouth. One day I pictured this patient as an infant injuring his mouth on a stony breast. I told him about it, and he was able to reflect. He wondered that he had never thought of that before. The pain stopped, a long time has passed, and there is no more talk of pain in the mouth, no grimacing, no need for a dentist.

I tried to find the words to describe what this patient went through and what I did to help him, but there are no words for this experience. Try as I do to tailor them to fit, they always fall a bit short. Will there ever be words for the vicissitudes of the milk and the suffering of the mouth? In the presence of the vastness of this phenomenon, I feel inadequate and sometimes frustrated. With what I do, nevertheless, hopeless cases have changed, recovered and taken their places in society. If only one other such gets well as a result of this book, I would feel that the effort is justified.

I am sure that the book has shortcomings and I console myself with the thought that I am still trying and hope to continue to try.

J. N. R.

New York City
November 1952

Contents

Direct Analysis: General Principles

I. Direct Analysis: The Psychoanalysis of Psychotics

DIRECT ANALYSIS is a psychologic technique having for its purpose the treatment and cure of psychotic patients. It began inconspicuously with a case described in my first paper, "A Method of Resolving Acute Catatonic Excitement" (Paper 2). The patient had arrived at a point called "exhaust status," a condition I had heard about but never seen. One could live a medical lifetime outside a psychiatric hospital and not see this condition. I came to the patient's room with curiosity rather than therapeutic zeal, but as I sensed the deadly threat of his psychopathology, I felt impelled by the strongest unconscious force to do something to help him.

It is important to the theory of direct analysis to emphasize that I had this unconscious impulsion to treat rather than any conscious determination to apply psychoanalysis to psychosis. It does not seem that the resulting treatment and its beneficial results follow the precise logic of medicine. The patient responds to some feeling which, if it exists, can be relied upon to cure. Who would suspect that man's humanity to man could be a medicine? It would be unfair to give this uncomplicated insight if the rest of the book were not devoted to amplifying it.

From intuitive beginnings, we have laboriously culled clinical data which we hope will bring this experience of feelings and the unconscious out into the light of day where it begins to make intellectual common sense.

The term "direct analysis" for this new therapy was originally suggested by Dr. Paul Federn when he discussed my second paper which I read in 1946 and later published under the title, "The

Treatment of Schizophrenic Psychosis by Direct Analytic Therapy" (Paper 3). I had sought Doctor Federn's help in unraveling with me the productions of various of my psychotic patients, and he became sufficiently interested to attend actual treatment sessions.

He expressed astonishment that nobody, to his knowledge, had ever before used "the method of *direct psychoanalytic* approach to the psychotic unconscious products," or had ever tried "to fight the complexes directly." I adopted the term "direct analysis" and in my early papers gave the impression that direct analysis simply meant direct interpretations. In the years since then, I have gained sufficient insight into the psychology of the unconscious to rationalize many of the techniques I had been using instinctively from the very beginning. From the innovation of direct interpretation, a whole complex body of knowledge has developed for which the term direct analysis is somewhat misleading. But in many ways the adjective "direct" characterizes my whole attitude toward the psychotic—the forcefulness, closeness and lack of formality. I have, therefore, continued to use it to refer broadly to the method I employ in the treatment of psychotic patients.

For terminologic convenience I will use "direct analysis" when referring to the psychoanalysis of psychotics and "analysis" (without qualification) when referring to the psychoanalysis of neurotics.

In its theoretic foundations, direct analysis is an extension of Freudian theory. Of necessity, the techniques have required radical innovations, inventions, and departures from ordinary psychoanalytic procedures.

The dynamics on which the technique of direct analysis is based comes from the dream psychology as formulated by Freud. Although this great doctrine was developed largely from the study and treatment of neurotics, Freud anticipated the extension of his therapeutic technique to psychotics when, in *The Outline of Psychoanalysis,* he expressed his hope that "the dreaded spontaneous illnesses of the mind" would eventually be cured.

Brill confirmed this latter-day hope of Freud when he wrote, in *Freud's Contribution to Psychiatry:* "Freud . . . did not at first advise analysis in such cases. He reasoned that as the dementia praecox process was itself a sort of adjustment, albeit morbid, if it were destroyed, the patient would be left without any support whatever. But when I discussed this problem with him later, I was pleased to learn that he no longer entertained this view. On the contrary, he felt that in time we would develop a psychoanalytic therapy for the psychoses."

So self-evidently promising did this hope of Freud's seem to me in my earlier days that I was surprised to learn that none of my psychoanalytic colleagues had attempted a systematic application of Freudian doctrine to the psychoses. In fact, at the hospital where I began my psychiatric training, psychoanalysis was taboo, even for what it could contribute to the understanding and custodial management of patients.

When I first started work with psychotic patients, my knowledge of psychoanalysis was limited to what I had learned in the first months of my personal analysis and from my reading on the subject. I was obliged to administer the standard physical therapies to the patients in my charge and, apart from that, all I could do for them was to listen to them. The more I listened, the more impressed I was at the similarity between psychotic material and dream material.

On the basis of what I had learned from carefully reading *The Interpretation of Dreams* and from carefully listening to my patients, I constructed the following simple hypothesis by which I felt the insights of Freud might be applied to the treatment of psychotic patients.

In the unconscious are the forbidden wishes which cannot come into consciousness because of taboos and threats of reprisal. The wishes gain limited gratification in dreams where, disguised through symbolization, condensation, displacement, and distortion, the images appear to be meaningless and innocent. The dreamer, thus kept by the censor from knowing the latent content of his dream, sleeps on. He wakes up if the dream censorship fails and the revelation of the real meaning of his dream becomes imminent. He may remember the details of his nightmare, but the dream is interrupted before he has had a glimpse of the forbidden wish.

In its manifest content, what is the psychosis but an interminable nightmare in which the wishes are so well disguised that the psychotic does not awaken? Why not then awaken the psychotic by unmasking the real content of his psychosis? Once the psychosis is stripped of its disguises, will not this dreamer too awaken? In my earliest work, this is what I did although it was only later that I understood it theoretically. In the course of my analysis, I discovered many times that my unconscious knew more than I did.

It is primarily in the therapeutic techniques of the analysis of psychotics that we depart from the usual Freudian techniques for the analysis of neurotics. The psychotic, unlike the neurotic, does not have the requisite maturity to follow the fundamental rule of free association. Nor can he be expected to lie down on the couch, nor to be satisfied with 50 minutes of the analyst's time each day. He cannot be expected to feel understood if the analyst remains silent, nor to have the courage to confront his terror if the analyst remains remote. Drastic changes in technique are required to meet the needs of the psychotic patient. The mute catatonic, for example, cannot free associate, but his gestures, expressions, and movements can be interpreted to him. The paranoid patient may have to be made to feel at the outset that the therapist shares all his suspicions. An anxious psychotic may have to be given immediately the reassurance which, for therapeutic reasons, is withheld from the anxious neurotic. The assaultive patient, who cannot be restrained by analytic rules, may have to be restrained physically. A man living in a nightmare cannot be handled like one with full consciousness and with all repressions in order. Although the fundamental dynamics are the same for neurotic and psychotic, the methods for dealing with them must differ.

Mental illness is a process in which various unworkable defenses are abandoned in the desperate retreat from reality. The individual is first neurotic, then at a deeper level is obsessive-compulsive, then manic-depressive, then paranoid, and only after these stages does deep psychosis develop.

The road back from psychosis appears to be the reverse of the road down. Advancing back from unreality, the patient works his way by stages to a neurosis resembling that which he had before. But much as it may be like the previous neurosis, it also differs from it. The revived neurosis has been modified by the whole experience of the psychosis and of the direct analytic treatment. To suggest this revival and modification we have invented the term "neoneurosis."

These papers, emphasizing as they do ideas, techniques, and case materials related to resolving the psychosis, may leave the reader with the impression that this is all the therapy needed to cure psychotics. I did think so at first; but within four years after I began my work, I found that a few of the patients whose psychosis I had rapidly resolved again became sick. Some of them I could still treat, and others, lost in the state hospital system, became chronic cases. I then recognized that, in order to secure the patient against a recurrence of his illness, it was necessary to follow the resolution of the psychosis with an analysis. It will be interesting to note that when this analytic phase really gets under way, occasionally violently charged transference material produces a brief transference psychosis. The important fact is that, although all other objects may again be lost, the patients do not lose me and are soon able to be analyzed again from the couch. Because the psychotic has experienced so much of the unconscious and has acquired such sharp insights from the direct analysis, the mandatory follow-up analysis is easier. Only with this further treatment can the patient be fully restored to health.

II. Direct Analysis: Concept of Psychosis

The premise of direct analysis is that, except in those cases where physical pathology can be clearly demonstrated, psychoses are psychogenic in origin and are treatable by psychologic means.

Freud's studies for the most part were confined to neurotic

behavior, but we believe he furnished the dynamics for all human behavior, from the psychotic to the hypothetic normal. We regard the neurotic and the psychotic as different only in degree or stage of illness; one is simply sicker than the other. I do not agree with those colleagues who maintain that because an individual becomes neurotic, he is therefore unable to be psychotic. Insofar as we all have an unconscious, we are all potentially psychotic. The more or less normal can become aware of their psychotic potential in dreams and through the psychopathology of every day life, the slips of the tongue, the forgotten name, the random, irrelevant thoughts. The admittedly neurotic is constantly warding off the unconscious in one way or another, by phobias, compulsive rituals, hypochondriasis. In both cases, the unconscious is held in check by mechanisms over which neither has any conscious control. Although it costs the neurotic tremendous amounts of energy to keep his unconscious where it belongs, he may succeed in doing so for a lifetime. But if pressure from within or without proves too great, the unconscious surges out, inundates the conscious, and the neurotic defenses give way to psychosis.

When the unconscious has finally broken through and remains broken through (psychosis), the patient's blocked wishes appear in the form of delusions, hallucinations, and other irrationalities. These blocked wishes may be for attainable aims, like incest, which are forbidden expression or are rendered anemic by the operation of the censorship, or they may be for impossible aims when, for example, the patient wants love from a nonloving mother.

Without listening to the psychotic patient long enough to hear his disguised complaints again and again and again, the healthy person can have no idea of the size and ramifications of this hidden world. We go beyond some of our colleagues who have stated that "schizophrenia" holds some secrets of the unconscious, and hold that *only* psychosis contains the key to the vastness and grandeur of the deepest levels of the unconscious. In the beginning, I half-heartedly agreed with the concept that the psychotic had undergone a regression to the earliest infantile levels. All I could hear, however, when I listened to patient after patient, sounded like the oedipal material that kept echoing in my mind in tune with my own analysis. Unconsciously, of course, I knew as much as any man's unconscious, but the level at which I was communicating with the patient was confined to the limits of my own conscious insights. The patient infantile? Yes, of course. He eats like a baby, he dresses like a baby, he soils and wets, and without a nurse he might very well starve to death. But the masturbation that was a common sight on all the wards and my patient who talked about having his mother "centered" were quite familiar to me, and I could easily say to myself, "Sure, masturbation and fantasies of incest." So I made genital interpretations and on more than one occasion I was punished for my ignorance by unrewarding direct analytic sessions.

Freud described how Schreber believed he was impregnated by the sun rays of God. Many patients talk like that, in genital images, and I made many interpretations at this level. The most that this will do is set the stage for improvement by demonstrating that you talk the patient's language, the language of the primary process. But now and then I made interpretations of anal cruelty and explosions, or its opposite, anal gifts of babies and wealth, with somewhat more success.

My progression from here on may be surmised. It was only when I could show the sun as the warm, loving mother, creator and supporter of all life, and her rays as the kind of milk that makes you fat and comfortable rather than pregnant that I began to get therapeutic responses from my patients that gave me a solid feeling. Furthermore, I began to understand, and never lose sight of the fact, that the wish for the warm impregnating sun that was Schreber's delusion would ultimately spring from the need to put this sun in place of the cold sun that made him insane. Every paranoid patient whose insides were rotted by bad food pointed the accusing finger at his destroyer again and again.

Lewin's theory of the dream screen and oral triad supported my understanding and broadened it. With a patient whose imaginary images disappeared after a long period of direct analysis, one symptom remained. Before his eyes there was an impenetrable fog or sometimes he called it a "cloud." If you could wipe away a normal dreamer's images, I'm sure you would see the same fog or cloud upon which they were projected—the maternal breast or its equivalent. Taking my cue from Lewin, I made a simple direct interpretation about the fog. No sooner did the patient grasp the meaning of what I was saying than the fog dissolved. He was now fully awake, and there was no obstruction to his vision. Those of us who witnessed this astounding episode gained a deepened conviction about the orality of psychosis, and this kind of concrete evidence is a strong support during the countless hours of seeming intangibility.

Psychotics live immediately under the shadow of the breast. This is able to tell us two things: first, the presenting aspect of their psychologic life is again the earliest infancy and, second, the nature of the breast upon whom they are so dependent threatens their life. This being so, how does Lewin's concept of the oral triad shed light on our problem? In health you eat, the breast eats you, you are warm within it, nothing to fear, you awaken again to its goodness. It will always be there. It has granted you omnipotence and as long as is necessary, it continues you that way. With another kind of breast, you daren't eat it. If it eats you, you will be ripped to pieces and destroyed, and how in the world can you possibly sleep? If you can sleep at all or if that is sleep, it is terrifying and we see this terror every day in our patients and their sleepless nightmare. It is from this experience that we learn the reason for the therapeutic response to oral interpretations. Just as the concept of neurosis as an oedipal problem becomes the cornerstone of analysis, so the concept of psychosis as an oral problem becomes the cornerstone of direct analysis.

III. Direct Analysis: Therapeutic Techniques

The governing principle of direct analysis is that the therapist must be a loving, omnipotent protector and provider for the patient. Expressed another way, he must be the idealized mother who now has the responsibility of bringing the patient up all over again. This duty must be undertaken because the patient has been forced, under heavy psychic threat, to become again for the most part an infant. Since direct analysis holds that this catastrophic collapse is the consequence of unconscious malevolent mothering, it could have been predicted, even in the absence of overwhelming clinical evidence, that the antidote would have to be a benevolent mother. We hold further that the unconscious of the infant is cognizant of whether or not its mother has the unconscious qualifications which allow her to be a benevolent mother.

The conscious, tangible needs of the patient which anyone can recognize, such as food, warmth, and protection, are the easiest for the therapist to provide. Much more difficult is providing the proper instinctual response which the benevolent mother must make to the unconscious needs of the patients. For this response, the therapist's own psyche must be in order. His instinctual drives of love, hate and aggression must have come into such a balance that, as he relates himself to the patient, the patient will thrive. This balance, representing the courage and maturity required to carry out the commands of the governing principle, cannot be forced by conscious effort alone. It is found in an uncultivated state throughout nature and sometimes can be acquired through the discipline of analysis. Successfully treated psychotics who have been analyzed always possess it. The delicacy of the perceptiveness which makes you aware of the needs of the patient as expressed by his manifest content is seldom preceded by the conscious question, I wonder what he means. The therapist knows what the patient means and finds confirmation of his knowledge in the happy consequences that result when his unconscious allows him to do what the patient is actually asking for. I do not say that my own instincts have always sustained me in relation to all cases, but exactly where I have come short, I have found out how indispensable the governing principle is. I and my co-workers have come to have great respect for the forces available to us from the unconscious that buttress and protect the therapy, frequently in the face of treacherous obstacles.

I used to wonder how my co-workers and I persisted with such devotion in the treatment of a slovenly, dirty, antagonistic and, all in all, physically repulsive person. I cannot say we do not react strongly to just these disgusting annoyances. We give vent to a considerable amount of anger and resentment, but holding us to our task is a loving instinct intensely stimulated by the knowledge that either we are right and win in the face of these odds or we are responsible for what will happen to the patient should he be sent to a state hospital, receive shock therapy, or suffer surgical destruction of the brain.

From the point of view of the patient, perhaps this very slovenliness is unconsciously created to make his withdrawal easier, since because of his dirtiness he will alienate the malevolent mother. The benevolent mother will bypass the conscious disgust and under the aegis of the governing principle will respond with healing libido.

There is another phase of this force in human psychology which, I believe, functions unconsciously and can aid the governing principle. It comes from the same root that determines the emotional irrationality of the idyllic fallacy. It works this way:

In the beginning, the patient is almost a stranger to you. You are indifferent to the stranger; you neither love him nor hate him. After the first interview, he may mean very little more to you than does the stranger, but you have already developed some feelings toward him whether good or bad. This is true of the disagreeable patient as well as of the agreeable one. As in all human relationships, the more time you spend with an individual, the less of a stranger he is and the more he means to you consciously and unconsciously.

When I was an intern in a general hospital, it was well known that the longer a good nurse worked on a case, the more attached she became to the patient. As a matter of fact, the termination of the relationship was an occasion for mourning and tears. Some of these nurses would frequently refuse a chronic case, knowing very well that time and "doing for" the patient would result in just this phenomenon: that they would become as attached to the patient as to a member of their own family.

Once the initial investment of interest, effort and time is made, the agreeable or disagreeable qualities of the patient are not the factors that sustain the therapist in his devotion. The patient has become like a member of your family and you have to respond to the needs of the patient on that basis. But there are other aspects in your relationship to members of your family. In no healthy family is love the only feeling. You begin to fight with the patient; you withdraw from the patient; you no longer make the same sacrifice for him. The therapist does many other things to diminish the intensity of the feeling after the needs of the patient have diminished.

I believe the unconscious implication of the patient being no longer a stranger to you and like one of your family stimulates certain unconscious ego interests related to identification. I think it means your family are like you; you are like your family; the more the patient becomes like one of your family, the more he is you. One of the motivating forces that compel you to do for a patient in some way has to do with the force that motivates you to do for yourself.

Treating a psychotic patient requires more than knowing what the governing principle is or telling the patient, "I am your idealized mother and will love and protect you." This would be as ineffectual as simple reassurance and we all know that it won't work. The way the therapist has to function in order to be the idealized mother is to do certain things consciously and unconsciously in such a way that the patient will understand that he is being loved, protected and provided for.

There were a number of different therapeutic maneuvers which I used on many occasions in the past and only slowly have I become consciously aware of them. I continue to use them at present and they have become so familiar to me that in the seminars, for the purpose of identification and communication, I have begun to call them by name. They are now quite well understood in the total scheme of my work. I am sure that there are many other practices which, although still outside of my conscious awareness, are part of my daily work with patients. They have one common tie, i.e., they all conform to the governing principle. Some of these contain harsh, aggressive, and stubborn attitudes toward the patient and it is not always easy to see in what way they are appropriate to the idealized mother.

Direct Interpretation

We consider direct interpretation our most important technique. It is the most effective way to gain the patient's acceptance of you in the complicated relationship which is to follow. The direct interpretations indicate to the patient that somewhere in his environment there now exists understanding, that it is magical, omnipotent understanding, the earliest understanding of him exhibited by an adult in his neonatal environment. In the majority of the cases, these interpretations plus your physical proximity to the patient quickly reward you by placing you within the patient's dream.

Direct interpretations differ significantly from the interpretations used in the analysis of the neurotic. Interpretations are made to the neurotic patient after he has learned from his therapist the meaning of symbols, dream interpretations, the associative logic of slips of the tongue and the affective consequence of the transference. Direct analysis does not require this preparation before making interpretations. It is as though the psychotic already knows what the neurotic goes to such pains to find out. The psychotic seems just about to know what the unconscious ego has been doing and why it has been doing it, and this preparation causes the patient to absorb the meaning of the interpretations as though there were no resistances.

The direct interpretation relates to the governing principle because it lets the sufferer know that his mumbo jumbo signals, like those used by the infant, are being understood. Gratification is more likely if somebody in the environment shows that he understands the wish and the need. Each little signal that is translated and each little wish that is gratified by the therapeutic exchange diminish by a certain percentage the great energy quantum that is being consumed to maintain the psychosis. Slowly, with each of these exchanges plus certain other additional therapeutic measures, the psychosis begins to loosen its grip and reality begins to seep in and show itself.

One of the working hypotheses of direct analysis is that in no case does the patient fail to produce or exhibit interpretable material. The patient must be viewed as being limited in making himself understood, as an infant has limitations in making known his needs. At any given moment, the therapist may be incapable of understanding and interpreting what the patient is saying or doing. But the important fact remains, that there always is meaning in the productions. The baby never cries without a reason.

The materials for interpretation are the verbal productions of the patient, his gestures, his mannerisms, his posture, his day to day conduct. These all add up to his manifest content. Direct analysis takes this manifest content and forces the patient to hear its latent meaning. Although the examples which are given below are primarily verbal productions, it should be emphasized that anything from a stomach rumble to an elaborate fantasy may be the material for interpretation.

When the patient is mute, he is generally rigid. In that case, it must be understood that what the patient is saying is "I am frightened stiff." You have to tell him just so that you understand this. It is necessary for the therapist to utilize that aspect of the hallucination, delusion, gesticulation, or whatever, to select that remark or act which, in the light of what we know about psychosis in general and this patient's psychosis in particular seems most obvious as expressing in this peculiar way some direct need of the patient. You must tell him what you see or hear him to be saying so that somewhere, inside of him, he will gain the sense that he is no longer alone; he is understood. Somebody is trying to understand, somebody is trying to help. Somebody will give him what he cannot get by himself.

I am just about convinced that the maximum therapeutic gain is achieved by gearing the direct interpretation to the oral level. Following are two examples:

A male patient felt compelled to discover a transmission which would be infinitely more powerful than all transmissions known to automotive engineering. After a little questioning it became quite apparent that the patient was using from his engineering background the idea of applying fluid to gain power and strength. His problem was how to transmit this fluid.

It was easy enough to understand this from a genital point of view as a transmission of semen, but the effect on the patient's psychosis was dramatic when we made an oral interpretation, *"How can you transmit mother's milk to your mouth?"* * The patient's confirmatory response was, "My mother thought I always needed a vacation." Therapist: *"Anything to get rid of you."*

The genital meaning of this fantasy is obvious. An incestuous genital interpretation could have been made. The therapist could have told the patient that he wanted a transmission as big and powerful as his father's so that he could transmit semen to his mother. An anal interpretation could also have been made. But only the oral interpretation gives a good therapeutic return.

A young female patient was brought to my office after many sleepless psychotic nights. She was hallucinating actively and asked, "What will happen when they discover what I have stolen?" I replied, *"If your mother wouldn't give it to you, you had a perfect right to steal it."* Here again the genital interpretation would have been, "You have no penis. You have to steal one." But the emphasis that had to be made in this case was that she had to find a way to surmount her mother's ungiving nature (breast). Later we were able to say, *"In struggling to gain mother's love and protection, you stole what you didn't have—something symbolizing a penis, hoping that possessing a penis, perhaps mother would love you."* This patient actually was a kleptomaniac before she became psychotic. During the analytic phase of her therapy, she came to understand that she wished to steal, not because of penis envy, but because if she had a penis then perhaps mother would love her.

* Analyst's remarks italicized throughout the book.

Transference Interpretations

The interpretations I have explained and illustrated thus far have been, strictly speaking, simple, direct interpretations. Many of the interpretations I make are not simple direct interpretations, but transference interpretations, in which I interpret the patient's behavior in terms of my emotionally charged maternal role as described under the governing principle. Frequently this type of interpretation has to do with some blatant behavior on the part of the patient which indicates a fantasy of being somebody or something which he is not in reality and has for its purpose the gaining of parental approval. A young man imagines that he is about to be married by the holiest father, even the Pope. He sees himself as being such an attractive young girl that no man can resist him. Having in this way warded off the incestuous possibility with mother now perhaps mother will love him. Understanding this, I forbade the patient to marry anybody but me, but then continued, *"I want you to be my son."* Almost a year later, when the patient's unconscious homosexuality came up in his analysis, he recalled this eposide in the psychosis and remembered what a relief it was to him when, through me, he accepted himself for what he was, a male.

Often female patients pull their hair out or cut their hair off as soon as they have an opportunity to do so. To these patients I denounce their act with fury, announcing that if they become a boy, I will hate them. As a man, I only love daughters. It is to be borne in mind that this does not complete the interpretation required for the girl who has snipped off her hair. I have to relate her act back to the mother in line with my understanding that if the patient is a boy, she will not be competing with her mother for her father, and then perhaps mother will love her.

In both these instances I take a parental role and with considerable feeling deny that I want either the boy to be a girl or the girl to be a boy and instead that what they are is what I want. If they try to be anything different, I'll hate them, not love them.

Aggression

Direct interpretations and transference interpretations free considerable quantities of energy. This energy was previously used to maintain the intensity of the psychosis. It will be observed that one of the first signs of a move toward reality is the patient's rapidly increasing aggression. It is our belief that this aggressiveness is fueled in part by the energy released. Having concentrated the patient's attention on the malevolent behavior of his real mother while he is still hazy as to who is who, the therapist often finds the full fury of this free energy turned against himself. At this crucial juncture, you are called upon to take certain risks, just like the physician who treats communicable diseases. However, you should keep these risks to a minimum by the use of available techniques of protection. With some luck and the willingness to accept a challenge, confronting and overcoming the patient's aggression presents you with the opportunity of turning this new development to his advantage.

The range of aggression is wide. You are frequently called upon to engage in an encounter which may require no more than that you out-glare the patient or stand your ground firmly as he assumes an angry, threatening attitude toward you, or you may actually be the victim of as much of a physical assault as the patient's strength makes possible. Sometimes you are in real danger, as I was in the case of R. Z., described in Paper 3. Ordinarily interpreting the aggression neutralizes these situations. Sometimes you have to match and overcome physical violence with physical strength.

When a patient is persistently and extremely violent, all psychologic measures may prove unavailing. Under those circumstances it is necessary to use the restraint sheet or the camisole. The patient's aggression must be brought under control. Just here is where one might doubt that our behavior follows the governing principle. We explain it in this way: the idealized mother must protect her child and sometimes this protection involves controlling his uncontrollable behavior. If she does not protect him and he cannot protect himself, whose responsibility is it that he must suffer talionic reprisal? If you protect him from his aggression, he will neither be punished according to the Mosaic law nor will he be called upon to suffer the unbearable guilt feelings that accompany rage and destruction directed against a love object. Use of restraint then will be similar to the physical overcoming of the patient mentioned above, and through both methods the patient learns that his aggression is nowhere near the world-shaking catastrophe that he envisioned. Furthermore, he takes another look at you with a new kind of interest, seeing you as a person who can protect him in the real world.

Treatment Milieu

Before we continue the description of other technical devices, it would be well to tell where these procedures are carried out. Ideally, the treatment milieu should be outside of a hospital in reasonably pleasant and safe surroundings. The ground floor is preferable, but if above the ground floor, the windows must be of shatter-proof glass or protected by metal grillwork that is artistic but safe. Granted safe surroundings and no need of physical re-straint, we rely on the surveillance of our aides to prevent the patient from harming himself or others. Depending on the case, this arrangement may provide a wide freedom or the freedom may be restricted, but the patient should not feel that he is a prisoner. The most significant advantages of this milieu are: first, the healthy effect it has on the patient's morale, and second, the oppor-tunity to adapt each aspect of the therapy to the patient's indi-viduality without needing to consider the group demands of an institution. The disadvantage, as with all custom-made commodi-ties, is expense. The cost is considerable. This is understandable because what you are doing in effect is creating an institution for one patient.

The key figure among the personnel required for this treatment milieu is the neoneurotic patient or the recovered psychotic who has completed his analysis. These former patients can hardly be called aides. More appropriate would be the term associate thera-pists, because, outside of the time I spend with the patient, their understanding and devotion continue around the clock. They are in charge of the other personnel which may number two, three or more, depending upon what part of the total time the patient has to be kept under protective surveillance. To keep a homicidal patient safe obviously requires two or three shifts of people per day, seven days a week. Although I employ trained psychiatric nurses, unless they have been analyzed or have suffered some kind of neurotic episode, they are least suited to help in direct analysis. I find that young graduate students who have majored in psychology and who have a strong interest in this kind of work are excellent psychiatric aides. They gain a surprising familiarity with the unconscious from sitting in on treatment sessions which I go to some trouble to explain to them in detail. I allow them to talk to me about their personal problems when these problems seem in some way related to the material we have worked through with the patient.

It seems that former psychotic patients provide more unconscious understanding and these interested psychology students provide more conscious know-how and, together, they offer the optimum protection and companionship for the sick patient.

Participation in the Psychosis

Sometimes early in treatment, sometimes late, there will come a break in the case where I and those who assist me recognize the constructive change in the patient's attitude toward me. I take this to mean that some of the patient's psychotic impregnability has given way and he is beginning to incorporate me into his psychotic world. This hard-won victory usually results from many arduous days of listening to the patient and forcefully making direct interpretations and transference interpretations. Sometimes this moment follows a violent physical struggle with the patient. Sometimes it comes from the glaring contest, mentioned above, from which the patient backs away. Sometimes nothing is said, but the patient turns deathly pale and a cold sweat breaks out on his face. With a mute catatonic, the patient may move his lips after they have been in a straight line for years and strain to talk.

Mumbled sounds may ensue. Sometimes it is none of these and all you can say is that your unconscious startles your conscious with the knowledge that that moment has arrived. The excitement and hope born of this moment when you find yourself added to the patient's delusions and voices makes it possible for you to continue and redouble your efforts. You have to be as ingenious and ingenuous as all nature in trying to help the patient in his new relationship to you. Every primitive resource in your make-up will be called into action as you, the loving, protecting, omnipotent mother, the idealized mother, who is now in the psychosis, pursue the patient in his desperate retreat from the mother he knew. Like the animal in the woods fleeing before a predatory foe, the patient fights with all the skill of his instincts. You the therapist, however, have an unconscious just like the psychotic that contains the elements of the phylogeny of ages past which will make available to you at least an equal cunning, guile, shrewdness, seductiveness and the other resources concerned with survival. The patient's unconscious and yours know the same secrets.

Misery Loves Company

One of the first devices I employ is to excite the patient's interest in a symptom he has hitherto violently denied.

A patient had successfully denied his psychotic behavior by insisting his trouble was malformation of the spine with an extra bone sticking out in back. He also had a most unusual springing step which he partly attributed to the spinal defect. On the day when I recognized that I was admitted to his psychosis, I was impressed by two new things in his attitude. He kept turning his head toward me instead of not looking at me as was his custom and when I asked him to let me feel his hand (cold and moist), he extended his hand to me whereas heretofore I could only examine it by force. Addressing my remarks to two other doctors and his nurse, I stated: *"Let me see, walking on my toes. I did that when I was crazy. What was it my psychiatrist said to me— oh yes, I recall. You're trying to be a woman. You walk as though you had high-heeled shoes on. But I don't believe in that non-*

sense. [To the patient] : *Would you like a cup of coffee? I think we have some cake in the house."* The patient remarked, "No, were you really insane, doctor? Did you really have that foot pull? It seems to pull up from the muscles of my leg. You never had a spine disease." I replied : *"Neither have you. A person who has been through your insanity understands these things, but enough of this psychology nonsense."* I then addressed myself again to the others, ignoring the patient's manifest interest in my alleged symptom. After a few minutes of talk about baseball and politics, the patient interrupted, "How can you believe that I want to be a girl?" I bade the patient good night, offering to shake his hand in leavetaking, but he withdrew it, stating, "I do that with ordinary people. I don't care to leave. You are the only one who has ever been sincere."

In every case where the patient persists in denying the existence of the psychotic basis for his behavior, when I can, I make believe I was once psychotic and had just those symptoms. The patient must face the fact that I am not now crazy. If I ever was crazy with those symptoms, I got well. Why shouldn't he get well too? If he thinks that maybe I'm lying to him, he takes it for a kind-hearted lie and many times after psychosis, with good humor and just a little ashamed, he will assert, "I knew it was a big lie. Maybe it wasn't true, but it surely warmed me toward you."

Magical Gestures

The patient cuts electric wires or smashes a radio. With the breakdown of the ego boundaries and the diffusion of mental geography, identities of the self and people are lost and time has become both now and then. In this state, the patient is plagued by visions and voices. The knowledge of now includes electricity and radio. They must be at fault. That's where the interminable messages come from. The patient, unrelieved by what he has done, turns to me with a look of appeal. With great solemnity, I make repetitious strokes through the air with my hand. I may jump at the air and shout. Sometimes I draw anti-witchcraft figures on a piece of paper and stick it on the wall. Always with a dead certainty, I announce that I have broken the rheostat or disconnected the voices. If the patient is intent on my performance, naturally he has withdrawn his attention from the hallucinatory experience. I claim credit for this and when I call his attention to the fact that the electricity stopped or the voices stopped or the images disappeared, he gains a feeling of my omnipotence, his anxiety diminishes, and I am ready to press my advantage. I am the omnipotent good mother. The electricity was the shock treatments of the patient's bad mother. The voices he heard were the grown-ups in the next room when he was a baby alone in the dark and frightened.

Becoming Figures in the Psychosis

Whoever the figure is that you become, whether it be an earthly parental figure such as the landlord or the president, or some heavenly figure like God or a planet, you must understand that invariably they represent mother. The patient, in catatonic excitement, threatened with loss of his life both psychologically and sometimes in reality, will, when the time comes, recognize your voice and face among the phantasmagoria of his psychosis. In a determined tone, you announce yourself as the omnipotent figure who has power of life and death over him but now is determined to wield this power only for life, that is, for the protection of his life (governing principle). With the mute catatonic, assuming his mental agony from what he says when he can talk (as in catatonic excitement), you make the same pronouncement. With this patient, however, after insisting that you are the good omnipotent figure, you force the patient to open his mouth by pressing firmly against his cheeks at the tooth line and when his mouth is forced open, you tell him to drink. *"The milk is warm and good. Not the poison that your mother fed you."*

A woman I am currently treating responded to this with the single word, "Bastard." I took this angry comment to mean annoyance that I was interfering with her psychotic safety. The fact that she did not die from my milk could be a reason why she obsessively scribbled my name innumerable times on a sheet of paper. This is the most response she has made to any environmental stimulus since she became ill many years ago.

The Trick against the Trick

The patient's delusion is a deception practiced for the purpose of gaining a remote or unobtainable object. His unconscious invents, lies, connives, disguises, and does magic to this end. When the delusion is finally organized, it may or may not be accompanied by anxiety. The absence of anxiety attests to a diabolic efficiency. So long as the delusional system remains so efficient, it interferes with movement toward the resolution of the psychosis. In this situation, as soon as possible, I employ a device called the trick against the trick.

The procedure must be carried out with assistants who are drilled in their parts. A patient believed her father was condemned to death in the state capital. I had the family foregather and produced a spurious reprieve from the governor. A celebration befitting such an occasion followed. The patient was dazed and participated in the celebration stiffly. Following this, she began to manifest anxiety relating to food and now she refused to eat for a period of time sufficiently prolonged to result in the loss of 40 pounds of weight. It can be surmised that the presence of Father again admitted the possibility of incest which might anger and alienate Mother. Mother would punish her with poison milk.

Accepting the Patient's Psychotic Reality

Certain paranoid patients think they are current political figures, great historical figures or divine religious figures. In order to have the patient who is always suspicious of you encouraged to abandon this suspicion, you act as though there is no doubt that they are who they say they are. Before Christ and the Holy Trinity you bend your knee and cross yourself. For Moses, Abraham and others, you become reverential in the tradition of the Old Testament. With presidents and generals you become grandiose about their greatness. Almost always the patient goes on and on expansively, giving you endless productions.

There is another class of paranoid thinking allied to this which makes the patient important from another point of view. I mean patients who think they're being spied upon by governmental agencies, congressional committees or giant corporations like the Telephone Company. I have in mind a patient who was able to get the attention of many important civil servants because she believed her telephone wire to be tapped and, to tease her, "they" played the conversations back to her, probably from a recording device.

One wonders why, in one instance, you tell a patient he's crazy and, in another, you make believe that what he says is real. Some clues suggest themselves, for example, a need to reduce the patient's suspiciousness or to increase his immediate comfort, but there are many instances where, much as I dislike conceding that I can be intuitively guided, I cannot more accurately appraise why I decide to accept the patient's psychotic pronouncements and let him go on rather than challenge them as I sometimes do. Usually I can point out what influenced me in the immediate content of the productions, but not infrequently I cannot. I am then forced to fall back for justification on the fact that the results usually show that my timing was good and I acted wisely.

The Return to Reality

As the various procedures which we have described bring the patient back toward mental health, the therapy undergoes an elevation of its sights. There is much less interpretation and much more adulation and support. It is entirely consistent with the governing principle that the child feel as loved at the age of 2 as he did at the age of 1½. As a matter of fact, various aspects of the idealized mother continue to operate in the maturing process of the child up to and including his beginning flights of independence and even after he sets up his own home and is a new and independent parent. The real parent will not thrill over the happy marriage and the happy parenthood of your former patient as much as you will. This general statement rather vaguely describes something about the counter-transference or your feelings toward the patient, who is now able to enjoy life adequately as he never could before. On the other hand I recognize more specific technical procedures applicable to the stage of therapy that leads the patient through the last phases of psychosis and into neoneurosis.

Before I describe these I would like to remind the reader that I am talking about the general rule rather than a rigid doctrine of treatment. Some things that I describe now may very well be used in the first treatment session and on some occasions a subtle direct interpretation is as applicable here as it was in the beginning of therapy.

The resistance to getting well is quite apparent here and throughout the neoneurotic phase but it is not as rock-ribbed as when you struggle to haul the patient out of the deepest recesses of the psychosis. Freud says a woman only gives up her penis envy after she has discovered joy in the genital that she was born with. In the same way, it is only after the patient has discovered a full measure of the happiness of maturity that he is no longer interested in or concerned with the phoney values of the psychosis.

Return to Reality (1): Reductio ad Absurdum. When the patient has been sufficiently freed from the toils of the psychosis to have the least bit of judgment and understanding, reducing his delusional content to absurdity may have a very telling effect on the whole illness. After struggling unsuccessfully with a young man for many months to get him to abandon his long hair and to change from his bizarre clothing to customary clothing, I resorted to force. He was no lightweight and it took four of us to hold him in the barber's chair. The following day, he was brought to my office minus the hair but still posing as Jesus Christ with a long flowing gray robe. I turned to his attendant and my secretary who was taking dictation and with some display of annoyance inquired: *"Isn't this the fourth Jesus Christ who's been here today? Let me see, there was Joe, he said he was Jesus Christ. There was Fred, he said he was Jesus Christ and then there was Milton, Dr. B's case—he said he was Jesus Christ too. The blasphemous nerve of these lunatics."* The patient listened to me and averted his gaze and I continued, *"I'll tell you what I'll do with you. If you promise to wear a pair of trousers tomorrow, I promise to buy you a new white shirt."* He shook hands with me and although he said nothing, I sensed that it was a bargain. Bright and early the next morning, I went to his apartment with the shirt I promised. The attendant had no trouble getting him to wear appropriate clothing. Apparently he was ready for this change and all that was required was to attack the delusional system as I have described. In addition to his symptomatic improvement, there was a general all-around improvement in his mental health. In a few weeks, he was able to lie on the couch and free associate, and two years later he was accepted as a student in medicine at one of the universities abroad. I ask myself here, How about the governing principle? I believe that the mother who has four children each of whom gets into similar mischief during the course of the afternoon, has a right to complain, "When will there be an end to this naughtiness?" and still be the idealized mother.

Reductio ad absurdum works well with patients who have made serious suicidal attempts. When they are well enough, their love of life is as strong as any man's and at least once I remind them of their act and portray it as the most ridiculous thing in the world because now what they did seems absurd to them, insofar as they would have killed themselves, not the hated image of the malevolent mother contained within. I am especially careful with such patients and I try to put as much distance between them and their suicidal wish as I can.

Return to Reality (2): Allowing the Patient to Act out. This is easy to do. It may be exemplified with a patient who ascribed to herself rank and power which was constantly seeking expression and to which I had made many interpretations over a considerable period of time. She was residing with one of my assistants at a mid-town New York City hotel. While I was denying her pretentious claims, she insisted that if she went into a restaurant, she could commandeer all the food there. I called her bluff and said, *"Go ahead and do it."* She went straight to the restaurant with Miss G. and myself hustling along. She walked into the restaurant —we stood at the door—and loudly she proclaimed that all the food belonged to her and she proceeded to take some boxes of sweets from a display counter. The waiters restrained her and the manager angrily called the police. When they arrived and the patient was thoroughly bewildered by this unfortunate turn of events, I introduced myself, informed the policeman that she was a mental case and quite harmless, and successfully prevailed upon him not to arrest the patient. One can readily understand that from that experience forward, the patient's belief in her omnipotence went into a severe decline. She was almost eager to listen to my explanations of this impetuous and uncontrollable urge to commandeer food.

Return to Reality (3): Handling Aggression. One can predict that with the beginning of the return to reality, the patient whenever possible will get into violent, sometimes physical altercations with members of his family. If I see this tendency developing, I take a firm hand as follows: *"If you ever again lay a hand on your mother, father, husband, wife, child, sibling* [whoever was put in jeopardy by the patient] *I will give you worse by far than you ever thought of doing to them. I forbid you to make any physical attack on a member of your family. If you feel you have to hit someone, hit me."* On rare occasions, patients have struck me or scratched me, but not seriously. The original fight that I described earlier in this section settles the issue of the patient's aggression toward the therapist, and the patient has no heart for repeating it. I must concede that the patient has plenty of justification for the rage and hostility directed against the parental figure who has been so traumatic. This may involve a great danger to treatment. Since sometimes without any excuse at all, a family takes the patient away from me just when reality is beginning, it would be foolish indeed to risk giving them any justifiable excuse because they do not understand that the patient's reprisal is unreal in relation to the present and is directed against the family of the past. The governing principle demands that the good mother protect her child from the evil that could befall him at the hands of the malevolent mother. What I hope to accomplish in addition is to force, by my counter-aggressive anger, the patient's attention back to me so that I may employ his affect to a therapeutic end.

Return to Reality (4): Re-enacting an Aspect of the Psychosis.
There comes a time when the patient no longer sees visions and
no longer hears voices. Also many other psychotic manifestations
that patients exhibit become weak or disappear. For a while, these
patients emerging into reality feel fuzzy and are fuzzy. It is like
moments of sleep just before you awaken. On certain days during the treatment, you know very well without tangible evidence
that the patient is shaky and could easily slip back a notch to
where he does hear voices. You do the following: *"Do you remember when you were crazy? You heard the voices coming from
over there behind the lamp. Now pay close attention. Look over
there. You hear the voices again, don't you? What are they
saying?"* The patient may be reluctant but you insist that he at
least make an attempt to hear the voices as he used to. You insist
that his denial is false, that he really does hear the voices and
try to get him to a pitch of resentment where with righteous in-
dignation he shouts at you that he does not hear the voices. At
this point you also know that the ego had some healthy exercise.
The patient is more likely to remain awake.

Some patients in the psychosis make explosive noises with their
mouths, jerk their bodies in an odd manner, pull out their hair in
certain spots, and indulge in other bizarre behavior. Whenever
your hunch tells you they are in danger of repeating some such
irrationality, you beat them to the draw by demanding that they
re-enact just exactly the piece of psychotic behavior that you fear
they may fall into again. Perhaps your boldness indicates to the
patient that you are willing to take a chance of making him act
crazy because you are convinced that he no longer can. Perhaps it
has something to do with the patient's sense of shame when you
ask him to do something foolish and remind him that he used to
do this foolish thing. Sometimes the patient makes an attempt to
re-enact the symptom which comes out very feebly, obviously not
spontaneous, and sometimes he will say he did it to humor you.
When the patient has clearly lost his touch, the therapist has
reason to rejoice.

PAPER 2.

A Method of Resolving Acute Catatonic Excitement

INDIVIDUALS SUFFERING FROM CATATONIC EXCITEMENT may develop a steadily mounting temperature accompanied by increasing exhaustion. These patients are ordinarily treated with continuous bath, sedation, supportive therapy, and forced feeding. The cases selected for this study had proved refractory to this method of treatment, and progressive exhaustion and loss of weight appeared to indicate a fatal outcome. The therapeutic approach instituted at this point was a psychologic one based on psychoanalytic concepts.

At the turn of the last century, catatonic excitement was known as "acute delirius mania," "Bell's mania," or "Bell's disease" and was considered an independent clinical entity. Kozowski [1], Redalié [2], Claude and Cuel [3], and others agreed that the symptom picture was one of disorientation, hallucination, elementary and generally confused intense motor activity, rise in temperature, and physical exhaustion with marked loss in weight. Death occurred in one to two weeks. Bleuler [4], Sander [5], Kozowski [1], and Binswanger and Berger [6] ascribed this fulminating illness to pathologic changes caused by autotoxic or infectious agents, while Thoma [7] thought it might be due to physical changes in the brain. Furstner [8], Weber [9b], Redalié [2] and Claude and Cuel [3] did not consider the brain pathology sufficiently specific to explain the excitement.

Subsequent studies proved these etiologic theories unsound. Scheidegger [10] and Fischer [11] concluded on the basis of clinical and autopsy findings that the illness was the result of a schizophrenic process and the cause of death the psychosis itself.

As opposed to the pure organicists, these men, who could find no pathology to account for the excited state, seemed more concerned with the content. As a result, their descriptions are rich and accurate in detail. They were particularly impressed with the fear exhibited by their patients. To emphasize this fear, they used such adjectives as—*hochgrädigster-angst* (highest degree of anxiety), *unheimliche-angst* (untranslatable), *wilde-angst* (wild anxiety), *triebmassige-angst* (driving anxiety). Schüle called it "demoniacal fear." However, one does not yet observe at this point any approach to the problem that may be considered truly psychodynamic. It remained for Freud and his followers to develop techniques and insights by means of which one may explore more profitably the content of mental states. The author has applied certain basic psychoanalytic concepts to penetrate the psychotic systems of individuals in acute catatonic excitement in an attempt to aid them to re-establish contact with reality through the medium of their contact with him. In order to establish such contact, the author deliberately assumed the identity, or identities, of the figures which appeared to be threatening the patient, and reassured the latter that, far from threatening him, they would love and protect him. If this seems to be a rather dramatic method and one calculated to arouse apprehension as to subsequent relations between the patient and physician, it can only be said that: (1) the patients who were selected for treatment showed mounting fever in spite of all the customary methods of treatment and seemed doomed to die, and (2) in no case did the outcome justify the apprehension.

The following are three of the cases treated in the manner described. All seven of the patients studied showed essentially similar responses.

Case 1

Joseph S., aged 15, was admitted to the New York State Psychiatric Institute and Hospital on January 27, 1943. He was described as moody, retarded, mute, and antisocial. He felt that everything was disintegrating about him and thought he was gradually "dying and evaporating." Voices called him vile and profane names but sometimes referred to him as a genius. Thyroid treatment was given from April to July, 1943, and he was discharged on August 31, 1943, as unimproved. The diagnosis was dementia præcox, catatonic type.

He was admitted to Brooklyn State Hospital on September 13, 1943, in a catatonic stupor with marked negativism and mutism and moderate cerea flexibilitas. On September 21, 1943, insulin shock therapy was begun, and he received a total of 42 treatments. Some improvement was noted. On November 2, metrazol shock therapy was started. After three treatments, he became increasingly excited and began to show elevation of temperature. Intravenous sodium amytal was effective for only a brief period in controlling his excitement. Finally, he was transferred to the medical ward where he was considered *in extremis*.

When approached by the physician at this time, the patient was in bed in a well-lighted room, protected by a restraint sheet. The physician took a position near the foot of the bed where he could easily be seen by the patient. The latter, who was straining against the sheet and rolling his head from side to side, looked feverish and exhausted. He said, "I didn't even touch him. The British Empire is coming to an end. The whole world is coming to an end. Where is that man? He just was captured. Looks like a fellow I once knew. You didn't do it. Well, I did it. Where am I now? Well, he's the man. He's crazy. Where is she? I didn't bother David Jay. [At this point the patient made a noise which sounded like that of an airplane motor. It will subsequently be referred to as the "motor noise."] I wouldn't mind finding a Messerschmitt. I'm surrounded. Help! Help! Did he yell?" This last is evidence of the degree of dissociation in this patient. He constantly referred to himself in the third person. To continue: "Why that American torture? Martial music. What's she picking up her leg for? Joseph S. He's the one. Where is that woman? My mother! All right, I'll have torture." These remarks appear to refer to an incestuous temptation. What the torture he referred to consisted of, or who was to administer it, the physician did not yet know.

What was noted, however, was intense fear and indescribable straining against the restraint sheet.

The physician shouted words of reassurance and encouragement to him but these were ineffective. In a few moments the patient continued: "He's coming at me. If I only had a machine gun. He's a Jew. Isn't he invisible? [Motor noise!] I only saw him in a picture. Long live the German empire. He's on top of us. Kill him, God damn it." The patient undoubtedly felt that he was in an airplane and that in his lofty position he was being threatened by disaster. "I should have been a girl." Apparently he was expressing a homosexual defense against incest temptations and the danger of the lofty position, i.e., manhood. "Can I kill him? Should I cut his head off?" At this point he again demonstrated a paroxysm of fear. "Oscar S. did it. [Oscar S. is his older brother.] Oscar and I used to fight. The British empire. They cut off my tongue." (Castration!) At this point the physician was attempting to understand the material in the same manner in which one follows free associations. Little was said to the patient, but it was surprising how clearly his problem revealed itself. The patient continued: "Go to Hell. God damn her. The son of a bitch. Who? My older brother. He's fighting for the American flag. I don't want an older brother. I wish Phillip A. S. was dead already. [Phillip A. S. is his father.] I drank a drop. I'm a baby." Treatment was discontinued, and orders were left for no sedation or tube-feeding. Sedation interrupts the productions and delays the next step in the treatment. Regarding the tube-feeding, the therapist wants the patient to be hungry, if possible, so that he may be spoon-fed by the physician in order to restore the early infantile relationship. It will be noted that the patient said he was a baby.

The second treatment was undertaken on November 13. The patient had spent a sleepless night and had kept on almost incessantly with the motor noise. His physical condition was so poor that the physician elected to enter his hallucinatory world dramatically in the rôle of father. In other cases, the physician assumed the rôle of priest, mother, mother-in-law, etc., depending upon the information gained from the productions. In this case, it appeared necessary to take on the father rôle before the indications for this step were clear, because the patient was rapidly getting worse. Since Oedipal material was preponderant and the patient appeared to feel that the father threatened his life, it was deemed necessary to show him that his father would protect his life rather than kill him.

When the physician entered the room at 10 a.m., the patient was making the motor noise: "Dracula. Let me go. My little brother. Trouble. Monsters." Again a paroxysm of fear. The physician said: *"I'm your father. Don't be afraid. Don't run away. I won't let anyone hurt you."* Thereupon he said: "He didn't say he loves her. I love who? Gorillas. You're right, Ma. I robbed a lot. World, I robbed. I'm proud of it. I spent it on a B-B gun. Phillip A. S., the dirtiest bitch that ever lived. Who the hell is Lewis S. He's crazy. Write that down." * (Note that this was the first remark directly addressed to the physician.) "So what? He robbed. Who's that? Joseph S. That's me. On top of the world. Would I kill that guy? Jerry's afraid of you. [Motor noise!] Oscar. Damn him. Oscar S. My grandfather. To think they tortured Ned. [Motor noise!] He's begging." The patient frequently referred to himself in the third person. Perhaps he was begging for mercy from a threatening figure. "Monster. Monster. Damn the American empire. Don't! Don't! Please! Oh, trouble! Patriot. Uncle Louis. Who the fuck is he? I'd murder him. My Uncle Ned died. Spencer Tracy. Who said noise?" (Motor noise!)

At this point, the physician held the patient's head in his hands and, speaking softly, told him that he was his father, that he loved him and would not punish him and that he would not permit anybody else to punish him. He then called him by name. The patient continued: "My name ain't Joseph S. He said he ain't Joseph S. Ned said he loved me. All that torture. How I love you!" Since the patient said "Ned [an uncle] loves me," the physician said *"I'm Uncle Ned. I love you. I will protect you.*

---

* I had a pad and a pencil and was taking verbatim notes.

Nobody will hurt you." The patient continued: "Louis too. Trouble, trouble. Oh, my mother. I don't want to touch her. No! No!" Here it was felt that if the patient could be made to understand that the physician understood his struggle with incestuous temptations, progress could be made. He was told plainly that the physician was his father and that he would not be punished even if he did it. He responded, apparently denying his incestuous wish, "I don't want to touch her," and made the motor noise loudly and for a long time. Apparently, he did not trust his physician (father). "No, no, no, no. I wanted to be a crook. Joe, don't go. Joe, I love you. I don't like the way my eyes see him. [Laughter.] Who are you?" (This was a direct reference to the physician, who thought it best to be Uncle Ned and said so.) He replied: "Ned W.? Where is he? I'm Ponce de Leon, Junior, restore youth. Are you Uncle Ned? You're not my Uncle. [Motor noise!] The monster. Where is he?" He was told that there was no monster present, and reassurances were repeated. Thereupon, he burst into gales of laughter. "She was a girl. She's a man now. The richest man in the world."

The patient made the motor noise, and the physician shouted to him: *"You can't get away like that any more. The plane doesn't work. It's broken."* He replied: "I love torture. No, I don't. Where is Uncle Ned?" The physician said: *"Here I am."* "You mean Ralph wants to fly a P-4. Let's go back. Quick. No. Ned, Ned. I'm not a woman. Where's Ned? He's gone." The physician interrupted with: *"No, I'm here. I'm Uncle Ned."* "Where's Oscar? Can I kill him?" As this question was directed to the examiner, it was assumed that he recognized the latter as a person with authority and power, apparently the beginning of evidence of a positive transference. He continued: "I don't want Rachel [his baby sister] in me." At this point, he made the motor noise which now seemed to be preponderantly a means of escape. When the material was of a threatening nature, he would use the motor noise to escape it. Here apparently, he was struggling with the fantasy of being pregnant, an identification with his mother. This might be construed as a defense against the passive homosexuality stimulated by the physician's assurances of love. Again, he was told that the plane was broken and that he did not need it anyway, since the physician would protect him against all harm. He went on: "Phillip A. S., my father. Oh, what trouble! Joe, I love you."

The physician pleaded with him: *"Let me help you."* This was greeted by the motor noise rather fiercely. "Died, did she?" The physician asked him: *"Who died, son?"* He replied: "Oh, he calls me son." The physician stated: *"Yes, you are my son. I love you. I'll take care of you. No one can harm you now."* The patient continued: "Cannon balls. That woman. No." The physician interrupted: *"I'll help you. I'll protect you."* The patient stated: "Damn it, damn it." Then, the motor noise. The physician repeated: *"It's no good any more,"* and the patient looked up and smiled rather pleasantly. He asked: "Where is Lou? The fucken bastard. I'll kill him. Lou said, 'Don't smoke.' You're going to die, Lou. Don't say that Joe. I still got time to live. She called me the freshest. My own mother. I'm a baby. Would I mind killing Ned? God, would I mind? Don't do it, Ned, please don't do it." Here, he showed intense fear, struggling constantly and making the motor noise. The physician kept up a steady barrage of reassurance, acting as the father figure, informing the patient that it was all a dream and nobody was hurting him. The boy went on: "Joe, I love you. I love Ned. Don't pity Joe. I restored her life by being a genius. I loved Anna. I grew up slowly —only six months. I had convulsions."

Between the ages of two and eight, the patient actually had had generalized convulsions two or three times a day, four times a week. What the patient said about growing up slowly could very well be evidence of beginning ego-strength. Perhaps he actually had the feeling of growing up as he emerged from the deepest reaches of the regressive phase of the psychosis. The physician stroked the patient's head in a reassuring manner, and he continued: "My mother's hand. God, get them away. Certainly, I'm dead. I'm a disgrace to East New York. Mary, I was never dead. Get away. Where am I?" The patient was told quite frankly: *"Brooklyn State Hospital—a mental hospital."* He replied: "Oh, a mental case. Who are you?" Answer, *"Dr. Rosen."* "Oh, Dr. Rosen. Phillip A. S." (The juxtaposition of his father's name with that of the physician appeared to indicate the acceptance of their identification in his mind.) "I don't know him. I only wish he would die. Set up the greatest torture—the greatest in the world. Why did he die? Oh, a weak heart. So easy."

At this point the patient was removed from restraint and the physician fed him soup, milk, bread and potatoes. He ate well and was quiet. This was the first time he had not been tube-fed in several weeks. He was told by the physician: *"That's a good boy. You ate well, Joe."* He replied: "Thanks, you bastard. You can't make me change my mind. [No great confidence in the father figure at this point.] Bertha S. [Mother.] That's the woman for you. Louis S. Don't let him live. I'm creating the end of the world. I'm a billionaire." (Motor noise!) Now the physician said to him: *"I know your secrets about your mother, how you hate your brother and father."* The patient interrupted: "That's right, that's right. My older brother too." The physician repeated his "secret," told him that he knew about his feelings toward his mother, but that he would, nevertheless, not be punished, that he would be protected against anything and everybody.

The boy listened with apparent attention and suddenly burst into tears, sobbing pathetically for some time. During this explosion of feeling, the physician was gentle, petted him, and told him that it made a big difference when someone was close to one and would fight for and protect him. He was told that he was just a frightened little boy. He made the motor noise feebly and not for long. He looked at the physician and said, "Get out of here or I'll kill you." Although he could hardly stand, he got off the bed and made violent attempts to attack the physician. The patient was again put in restraint, and the physician left the room for a while. During this time, the patient remained completely quiet. When the physician re-entered the room, he showed a dollar bill to the boy and questioned: *"What is this, Joe?"* He replied: "One dollar." The doctor answered, *"Correct."* He remained calm and smiled at the physician rather shyly. He appeared to be reassured but frequently took flight into psychosis. From time to time he grinned at the physician. After this period of being "a good boy," he was again released from restraint. He became excited and whispered to himself but calmed down. He was told that there was no need to run away, that from now on he would always be protected. He then broke into profuse perspiration, and when his temperature was taken shortly afterward, it was normal for the first time since his admission to the medical ward. Except for a half-hour, the physician was with the patient continuously for 16 hours and did not leave him until he fell asleep. The boy then slept, with few interruptions, throughout the night.

From this point on, the patient improved rapidly. He began to mingle with the other patients, took care of his personal wants, and became quiet and tractable. He was strongly attached to the physician and referred to him as his doctor, showing no tendency to identify him with the rôles which had been assumed by the latter.

Some months after his admission, the patient was paroled from the hospital and was subsequently able to maintain himself at a fairly good level.

Case 2

Mary B., married, aged 27, was admitted to Brooklyn State Hospital on October 18, 1943. She had been well until 1937, when in the sixth month of a pregnancy, she became mute, rigid and inaccessible. After delivery, the patient had remained mute for six months. She gave birth to a second child in August, 1943, and a few days later became confused and complained of visual and auditory hallucinations. She became so disturbed at home that hospitalization was requested.

She was diagnosed as in a catatonic exhaustion state on October 28, and the usual treatment of sedation and forced feeding was instituted, but to no avail. She continued to be excited and toward the end of the following month began to show an elevation in temperature. On December 7, the physician was asked to undertake the treatment of this patient since she was considered to be in a state of exhaustion. Her first significant productions were as follows: "The murderer is Sylvia A. [her mother-in-law]. This is a dead grave. Who drops dead all the time? My mother-in-law is a dope fiend. Jealousy? I ignore everyone. Thou shalt not kill. My murder-in-law. Lottie is my child. I killed her to relieve my mother, Sylvia. The bitch murdered even God. Roger died. My mother-in-law murdered Roger." There is no need to report all the productions, but it may be mentioned that the assumption by the physician of the rôles of mother-in-law, husband, mother, or father made no impression upon the patient. Finally, the physician told the patient: "*Sylvia A. did not kill God. I am God. I am here to help you. I will protect you against your mother-in-law.*" The patient demanded "Put my mother-in-law in the electric chair. She murdered my entire family. I outwitted her. I am fighting her. It is very hard. She kills God. Get rid of that woman. Who are you?"

This was the first contact, and it was maintained, although again and again the patient made references to the mother figure as a murderer to the accompaniment of obvious expressions of terror. After much assurance that the physician would help her fight her mother-in-law, she finally replied: "Oh, thank you. YOU can't protect me." She was again reminded that the physician was God and that he could protect her from anything. The woman said: "That is a confusion, a difficulty. I know my mother-in-law." She was removed from restraint and requested cereal, milk, and ice cream which were fed to her by the physician. She declared: "You will have to kill that killer-diller Sylvia. She is a bitch. What a job. I could never control her. I would like to kill my mother-in-law. By the way, is there still a World War going on? Today is Angel of Mercy Day. My mother-in-law controls the entire world. She picks up graves. Give her the electric chair." The patient was again reassured about the physician's ability to protect her from her mother-in-law and was told that she need have no fear of the world now since there was someone who could take care of her. She said: "That would be swell. I threw out my husband and brother. You have to be my husband. You have to protect me. I am getting **knife stabs all over.**"

The young woman warned the physician to be careful of her mother-in-law as the latter would kill him and was told again not to be afraid since the physician had the power to prevent her from killing him. The patient was released from restraint, and shortly afterward her temperature was found to be normal. It remained so. The physician spent the following two days with this patient. On both occasions, she was in contact but showed quite clearly the schizophrenic involvement. Her condition remained unchanged until she was recommended for parole on March 25, 1944.

In this case, it was found necessary to assume a rôle which transcended that of the usual authoritative figure, possibly because the patient's fear and hatred of her relatives, as the productions clearly indicated, was so intense that she could not experience enough positive feeling for them to give a modicum of security to her.

Case 3

Daniel K., 22 years old, was admitted to Brooklyn State Hospital on September 20, 1943. The diagnosis was schizophrenia, catatonic type. The young man was of average intelligence, had completed two years of high school, lived with his father and married sister, and worked in the trucking business. He had been inducted into the army on November 7, 1942 and discharged five months later for a "neuropsychiatric" illness. Four months after his discharge, on August 23, 1943, he had stopped working and complained that his mind was separating from his body. On October 4, two weeks after admission to the hospital, the patient became excited and was placed in restraint. He talked continually without paying any apparent attention to questions. The content was chiefly of a sexual nature.

The physician saw him for the first time on October 11, when he presented the usual picture of catatonic excitement with impending exhaustion state. There had been a marked loss of weight and a sharp elevation in temperature. He was tearing furiously at the restraint sheets, and his face presented a picture of intense fright. For the first hour, his productions were repetitious and revealed that he was actively hallucinating. He made reference to numerous sexual adventures. He spoke as follows: "This is a wonderful airplane. It's over the Atlantic Ocean. I can see her down there. My mother. She's floating. Here I go. A dive bomb. I have her centered. Here I go. Here I go."

Following this symbolic incestuous experience, the patient screamed in terror and appeared to plead for mercy with his father. "Don't cut off my balls. Please don't cut them off. Please, papa, please." Since the plea was directed toward "papa," the physician said he was "papa," that he had seen what happened, and that everything would be all right. The patient received permission to have these thoughts about his mother and was promised that there would be no punishment. He looked up, obviously incredulous, and replied, "Go ahead. Sock me, sock me." When assured that he would not be hit, he said, "I don't believe it."

The young man became much calmer after this exchange and continued so for some time. There was an abrupt and dramatic diminution in productions and excitement. As with the other patients, he was removed from restraint and fed by the physician. Three hours later, his temperature was taken and found to be normal. During the ensuing four days, he remained free of excitement and was partially in contact with his environment. In the course of interviews, he admitted that he was terribly afraid of going out into the world again and leaned heavily on the simple reassurances given to him by the physician. As soon as any degree of contact with the physician was obtained, the fictitious rôle of the father was given up; and, as with the others, the physician was referred to as "Doctor." The strong positive transference, however, was carried over, and this patient said: "Please, doctor, if you stick with me I will do anything in the world for you." About two weeks later, an interesting event occurred in this case. During the interview, the patient suddenly stood up and declared, "I am going to kill you." The physician asked, *"Why would you want to kill me? Why would you kill anyone who loves you?"* The patient then began to cry and said that he had to threaten to do so in order to make certain that the physician really loved him. His tenseness subsided, he grasped the physician's hand and kissed it repeatedly and pleaded to be taken care of. Such a childish attempt at reality-testing is a good prognostic sign. Psychotherapy was continued until November 23, when Daniel K. was paroled and told to report once a week. He found a job, earned an excellent salary, and lived at home with his father and married sister. At first, he called the hospital several times a day to complain bitterly that his father was constantly threatening him. With the assistance of a social worker, he obtained lodgings elsewhere, has since been working steadily, and is making an adequate adjustment.

Discussion

Psychoses and dreams, or perhaps more correctly psychoses and nightmares, have much in common. Freud pointed this out in the *Interpretation of Dreams* [12]. The material they both make use of comes from the unconscious system, and, while the psychotic and dreamer are thus hallucinating, the function of the conscious system is lost. In both states, the ego is woefully weak. But psychoses are not literally dreams, and it is pertinent to ask what prevents the psychotic from waking up like the sleeper. In the dreamer, the weakening of the ego is a physiologic process which is reversible, while, in the catatonic, the weak ego is the result of pathologic deterioration. The successful dream safeguards sleep and overcomes anxiety through the assistance of the pre-conscious. In the nightmare, the dream fails to succeed by these means, but, on waking up, the psyche has at its disposal all the reinforcements of the conscious ego so that life can go on in a relatively normal way. In the excited catatonic, we deal with a continuous nightmare from which there is no waking up, inasmuch as the conscious ego, which would have to come to the rescue, consists of remnants or shadows of the normal ego and perforce must fail the sufferer.

The catatonic state is one of nature's defenses, to be sure, but, for inefficiency, it must be classed with hyperpyrexia in an infectious disease or with post-operative paralytic ileus. The defensive symptom then becomes more threatening than the illness itself. Since the symptoms are a defense against the disease, which in turn is a threat against life, where is the psychopathology located? How is the life endangered? The answer to these questions is to be found in the behavior and the products of the patient. The illness seems to be built around the general theme of fear. This fear is an enormous one, because, as the productions reveal, the patient anticipates murder at the hands of an infantile love object. As has already been stated, earlier authors who described this condition were aware of this fear, but lacked a method for understanding it, so that this symptom was not accorded the investigation which it rightfully deserved.

Applying the concept of this intense fear as our basic one, we are better able to interpret the counterpart of catatonic excitement, the catatonic stupor state. Here one finds the patient securely withdrawn into a *sanctum sanctorum*. He is mute and out of contact. The implication is obvious. He does this to get away from somebody. Running away implies the existence of danger, but, while the patient, by retiring into a stupor, is safe enough from his fancied enemies, he also becomes walled off from his would-be friends. When he is excited, however, the yearning for human contact and understanding has broken through his defenses, and he tries to tell us something. He wants to come out if he dares. His excited productions are thoroughly disguised, but they are something to work with, a break in the armor through which we can pour our therapeutic endeavors, or more correctly, our ego and ourselves, with dynamic force. Perhaps one may take the liberty of calling this an ego "transfusion." At any rate, the strong ego of the physician serves as a support for the weak ego of the patient. The problem, then, is one of supplementing a sick ego with a healthy one. The physician must lend himself to the psychosis in such a rôle that the patient will finally trust him in order to leave his retreat for the world of reality.

Returning again to the dreamer, his problems, if he is neurotic and under treatment, may be handled in a leisurely way. There is adequate time to wait for associations which clarify the dream and prove the hypothesis. In the excited schizophrenic, on the other hand, one is constantly faced with the specter of the exhaustion state. This is a very real danger to life and one which permits no loss of time. One must, therefore, take certain liberties which psychoanalytic technique ordinarily forbids. The therapist becomes the surgeon confronted with the need for heroic surgery. At this point, it is necessary to refer to the concept of narcissistic regression in schizophrenia. This is so deep that the patients again live in a world of magical figures. The productions tell which of these the patient mortally fears. One must try to personify his terrifying images and convert them into protecting images. These, the patient can project upon a real object, the physician. This means the rapid establishment of a strong positive transference with a growing confidence which becomes the bridge to reality. Many other workers have demonstrated that the schizophrenic is capable of such transference.

The unconscious material and the symbols represented must be directly translated into the language of the secondary process. To a certain extent, this becomes a matter of trial and error, and many misinterpretations are made to the patient, but these appear to do no harm. The correct interpretations, however, strike deep and bind the patient to the therapist and to reality rather effectively. There is ample proof of this in the furious fight that the patient puts up to escape the physician as he finds himself irresistibly drawn to areas where there exist the dangers he originally sought to escape. The doctor's tools, then, are the transference and the dynamic interpretation. The objective is to gain and maintain contact with the patient through his visual and auditory pathways. These avenues, it seems, he cannot block out. The source of mental excitation is the stimulus coming from within, and from this there is no escape. The source of the internal tension must be understood and changed in order to obtain relief and quiescence. In the case of Joseph S., his dread sprang from the timelessness of the unconscious. It was a direct Oedipal situation, and his fears of death at the hands of the primitive father were just as real to him as to the savage described in *Totem and Taboo*. It is hardly a coincidence that in such a succession of cases, there should be revealed so simply and directly this fear of death. It is no wonder, then, that the reprieve and the protection from the substitute infantile love object produce such prompt and tremendous relief. That it requires more than the administration of sympathy to relieve this state was fortunately proved by the fact that the nurse in charge of these patients happened to be a tender person who constantly ministered to these sufferers with the utmost kindness.

Summary

A rapid method of psychotherapy for patients in acute catatonic excitement, sufficiently effective to relieve cases in exhaust status, is presented. It is essentially based upon a dramatization by the physician of the rôle or rôles of one or more of the infantile figures which appear to threaten the patients with death. It is suggested that this method derives its efficacy by establishing a symbiotic relationship between the weak ego of the catatonic and the strong ego of the therapist.

References

1. Kozowsky, A. D.: Zur Pathologie des Delirium acutum. Allg. Z. Psychiatr., 68:415–428, 1911.
2. Redalié, L.: Contribution à l'étude de l'anatomie pathologique du délire aigu idiopathique. Schweiz Arch. Neurol., 7:35–48, 1920.
3. Claude, H., and Cuel, J.: Notes anatamocliniques sur trois cas de délire aigu. Encéphale, 22:628–632, 1927.
4. Bleuler, P. E.: Dementia præcox oder Gruppe der Schizophrenien. (In) Handbuch d. Psychiatrie. (Anschaffenburg). Spez. teil., Abt. 4, Hälfte 1. Leipzig, Deuticke, 1911.
5. Sander, M.: Beiträge zur Aetiologie und pathologischen Anatomie Akuter Geistesstörungen. Arch. f. psychiatr., 34:490–522, 1901.
6. Binswanger, O., and Berger, H.: Zur Klinik und pathologischen Anatomie der postinfectiösen und Intoxikations Psychosen. Arch. f. psychiatr., 34: 107–139, 1901.
7. Thoma: Beiträge zur Klinik und Pathologie akut letal verlaufender Psychosen. Allgem. Z. Psychiatr., 66:737–758, 1909.
8. Fürstner: Über delirium acutum. Arch. f. psychiatr., 11:517–531, 1881.
9a. Weber, L. W.: Über akute tödlich verlaufende Psychosen. Monatsch. f. psych. u. neurol., 16:81–98, 1904.
9b. Weber, C.: Anatomische Befunde bei akuten Psychosen. eit. f. d. ges. Neurol. u. Psych. (Referate u. Ergebnisse) 7:413, 1913.
10. Scheidegger, W.: Katatone Todesfälle in der Psychiatrischen Klinik von Zürich von 1900 bis 1928. eit. f. d. ges. Neurol., 120:587–649, 1929.
11. Fischer, Johanna: Todesfälle bei akuten Katatonien. Leipzig Thesis, 1934.
12. Freud, S.: The Interpretation of Dreams. London. Allen. 1913.

The Treatment of Schizophrenic Psychosis by Direct Analytic Therapy

THIS PAPER is an attempt to describe—with an illustrative case history—the method the writer has employed in the apparently successful treatment of 37 cases of so-called deteriorated schizophrenia. This group included the three chief categories that are used diagnostically, hebephrenic, catatonic, and paranoid. I wish frankly to admit that it is not at all clear in my mind what the fundamentals in this method are, but I have every reason to believe that the foundations upon which this therapy is based, although still obscure, are nonetheless sound.

An absolute essential in the equipment of the therapist is the deepest possible knowledge of the unconscious. It will soon be seen—when I describe what actually goes on between the patient and myself—that I was called upon to converse with the patient in the language of the unconscious and to be in a position to interpret the unconscious to him at every single available opportunity.

Each symptom, each remark, every symbol must be untwisted, clear down to its earliest ontogenetic and even philogenetic roots in the unconscious. Only when the symptom is so clearly unmasked to the patient that it will no longer serve its purpose, will he be able to relinquish it for a more sensible way of handling his instinctual drives. The task is not completed with the resolution of the psychosis and can only be considered concluded when the transference is as completely worked out as we aim to do in ordinary analytic procedures.

I have shown in the preceding paper that an empiric procedure resulted in an enormous diminution of the psychotic anxiety. It was this simple discovery of talking directly to the unconscious, which was incidentally the only mental activity operating in those patients, that gave me the hope that some kind of elaboration of this formula might succeed in more chronic cases where the "scar tissue" and other evidences of pathologic repair were in greater abundance.

Early years of training in pathology prompted me to describe the deteriorated schizophrenic in these organic terms, although at no point along the line have I ever been persuaded that there exists in these patients an organic or even constitutional factor that could begin to fulfill the criteria of Koch's postulates. In each case, in accordance with well-known authors, I also found environmental factors of such distressing intensity that, if they could be duplicated, I believe they would produce the same type of psychosis in many other individuals as that which was produced in the unfortunate victims.

Before giving excerpts from the treatment of an apparently deteriorated schizophrenic of the paranoid type, it must be said that the method must be modified to meet the needs of each individual case. For instance, one of my patients in a catatonic state never uttered a word to me over a period of nine months, whereas a hebephrenic of many years duration hardly ever gave me an opportunity to get a word in edgewise. I believe, however, that something in the therapy is common to all.

In the case of the hebephrenic, the words "gotten in edgewise" finally had effect. In that of the catatonic, the words cast into an apparent vacuum proved to have taken effect. The patient, a married woman in her late twenties, spoke at last. The physician had tended her, fed her, treated her like a baby for nine months. For two of them, he had been with her for 10 hours a day, for the next seven, for four. When she started to improve, her progress was rapid. Today she has been well for a year, making an adjustment far above her pre-psychotic level. She is mature in relations with her children, against whom she formerly had much unconscious hostility, and is active in child study association work. She has taken charge of her own family affairs and has forbidden her mother to shop for her, as the older woman formerly did. She has asserted her independence to her husband who, as a result, thinks more of her than ever. Her pre-psychotic sexual relations were in obedience to her husband's demands and performed with very little feeling; she now has intercourse frequently and on a mature level and with normal enjoyment of both fore-play and intercourse itself. Formerly shy and schizoid, she now has many friends and leads an active social life in which she generally dominates.*

In 36 of these cases, the psychosis was resolved. The thirty-seventh patient, still psychotic,† has been with me for eight weeks. Some patients have been discharged as "recovered," and others are still in analysis. One of the patients, after a two-year lapse of time, and while still being analyzed, again manifested psychotic behavior. The immediate cause was a suicidal attempt by her sister, who was very dear to this patient. The patient is now being studied to determine to what extent her insight altered the present picture. The impression I get from her at this time is dilemma and confusion rather than the deteriorated psychosis she originally had.**

Regarding recovered patients: Let me define "recovery." As I use this term, it does not mean merely that the patient is able to live comfortably outside an institution, but rather that such a degree of integrity is achieved that the emotional stability of the patient and his personality and character-structures are so well organized as to withstand at least as much environmental assault as is expected of a normal person, that is, of a person who never experienced a psychotic episode.

* The editor of *The Psychiatric Quarterly* and three other members of the editorial board saw and interviewed this patient, both formally and through ordinary friendly conversation. The editor agrees, and his three associates concur, that Dr. Rosen's description and evaluation of his results represent what actually occurs.

† The psychosis of this patient has been resolved since this was written.

** The relapse lasted only a few weeks and the patient is now back at home and free from psychotic symptoms. She shows evidence of having gained insight as a result of this pseudo-psychotic experience.

The findings to date are empiric ones. They are expressions of some natural law of human behavior, just as surely as thunder and lightning are expressions of a natural law. At the present time I cannot come up with the right answers, but there is no doubt that they exist. Freud, Federn, and others have indicated the existence of general psychodynamic laws in their theoretic concepts of the ego, the super-ego and the id. When the gaps in this knowledge are filled, the secret of the etiology of schizophrenia will be revealed.

The diagnoses of schizophrenia were in all cases made by physicians other than the present writer, in most cases concurred in by more than one physician. Because the question of diagnosis is certain to be raised by a presentation of this sort, the writer has purposely excluded from this report four other cases—also diagnosed schizophrenia by other psychiatrists—but in which he feels the symptomatology was mainly manic-depressive. It has been the aim, in investigating the possibilities of this therapy, to treat initially only patients who were severely schizophrenic beyond the possibility of a doubt. It should be said that the four where the writer found manic-depressive features have made apparently complete recoveries also.

Honi Soit Qui Mal y Pense

This paper is in large part a clinical report dealing with the treatment of a single patient. Unavoidably, it reports the patient's language—his exact language. The language of schizophrenia is often offensive. Although the psychotherapist must learn neither to take nor to feel offense, it is only fair to say that there is much reported here which even the professional reader will find startling and revolting. But to disguise it with the euphemisms of scientific terms would be to distort the whole picture inexcusably, to present it with an air of unreality, to rob it of affect. It would be a complete misrepresentation to say that having had a spoon put in R. Z.'s mouth reminded him of fellatio; it did not; it reminded him of "cock-sucking." And it would be even more of an absurdity to say that the patient told the physician to have intercourse with himself, to avoid the belligerent, affect-laden command, "Fuck yourself!" The writer feels, nevertheless, that there is so much of this material that he owes even the psychiatrist reader this note of warning and apology.

Case History

R. Z. (No. 37 in table 1), aged 49, is a single, white man, born in New York City. He attended grammar school and is a Protestant. He is a tall man, well-built, and physical examination reveals no abnormalities. His anamnesis is sketchy, because his talk was scattered and his orientation was poor. He came to me because he heard voices and he could not work. The voices started in 1922 and were still with him. In 1922, the voices told him to join the Masons, to get an apron, and then to hell with it. He accounted for the voices on the basis of some form of electrical telepathy. During the previous four years, on and off, he had been at a mental hospital, where he had had a series of electric shock treatments and then a series of insulin. What was most disturbing to him were attacks of pain throughout his body which he called "those terrific seizures."

There were two voices particularly familiar to him. The principal voice was a woman's. Whatever he did had a special meaning, but just what that meaning was, he didn't know. He was vague about his past life and his family. His parents, Austrian-born, and emigrants to this country, were both dead. He had a very hazy recollection of them and of when they died but thought they were kind-hearted persons. He has two siblings, the older, a brother, whom he hasn't seen in he "doesn't know how many" years, and an older sister, who is married and lives in Texas. The first session was disappointing indeed. During an hour's time, he spoke only once: "Suck my ass.* Kiss my ass. I am not afraid of anything."

On the following day he seemed somewhat more relaxed and was able to sit still in the chair. He said: "Open your mouth." (The analyst): *"Who told you this?"* "I can't be sure. A voice."

* Arse.

"What does it mean?" "To suck a cock." *"Do you?"* "No, I never did." *"Did anyone do it to you?"* "No, I remember before I went to school, I was very young, some one took me into the cellar and gave me a bag of candy. I have never felt ashamed of it. I lived through plenty of misery and pain for it. When I was 11, some kids were playing 'dog' with their 'pricks' out, lapping each other. They asked me to play. I did. One of the kids did it for me, and I gave him presents and then money. I liked the sensation. It started me off with masturbation. Some years later at a bar I met the boy. After I had a few beers, I offered him 50 cents. He said if I didn't leave him alone he'd tell his mother. I forgot all about those things until 1940."

Bearing in mind what Freud teaches us about the homosexual aspects of paranoia, it was simple enough to interpret, "Open your mouth." Although the patient had at first denied his homosexual tendencies, he apparently poured forth considerable material indicating them.

The physician assumed a permissive rôle and acted as if he didn't understand why the patient was worried. The analyst said that many persons had homosexual experiences, especially children, and he added that he recalled stories of "things like that" where he was brought up. The patient made a point of denying any interest in this type of sexual activity but indicated that he was constantly suspicious of persons who went into subway toilets. For many years, he was a motorman on a subway train, and he remembered tales told by guards of how they made a lot of money by letting fellows "do that" to them. If he had wanted to, he could have made plenty of money "that way." The patient left the interview apparently greatly reassured, and the writer learned something that he didn't ascertain from the history, namely, that the patient had been working as a motorman.

At the next interview, R. Z. stated: "Open wide. Hold your breath. Don't be afraid to tell him it. The voice said: 'Piss on your mother's grave. Kiss my ass. Don't say that.' " What he ascribes to the voice here is his own Oedipal fantasy, and it was not surprising that his associations had to do with intercourse.

TABLE 1

Summary of 37 Cases Treated by Direct Analytic Therapy *

Patient	Sex	Marital status	Age	Diagnosis	Symptomatology	Duration of psychosis	Total hospitalization time	"Shock" Treatments Type
1	F	M	34	Schizo-phrenia	Depressed, anxious self-centered, retarded	7 mos.	9 mos.	ECT Insulin
2†	F	M	27	Schizo-phrenia	Confused, visual and auditory hallucinations, excited, temperature rose shortly after admission	6 yrs.	5 mos.	Unknown
3	F	M	31	Schizo-phrenia	Contact superficial, sentences disconnected and illogical, blocking, depressed, fearful, crying, visual and auditory hallucinations, feelings of unreality and depersonalization	2 yrs.	6 mos.	ECT Insulin
4	F	M	41	Schizo-phrenia	Profound depression, bizarre and illogical ideas, archaic thinking	11 mos.	11 mos.	ECT Insulin
5	F	S	34	Schizo-phrenia	Depression, obsessions, auditory hallucinations, periods of excitement	5 yrs.	5 yrs.	ECT ECT with Insulin
6	F	M	43	Schizo-phrenia	Claustrophobia, confusion, fear of homicidal intent, delusions, agoraphobia	16 yrs.	None	None
7	F	S	31	Schizo-phrenia	Vague anxiety, headaches, insomnia, depression, inability to work	6 mos.	5 mos.	None
8	F	S	22	Schizo-phrenia	Excitement, overactivity, assaultiveness, hallucinations, screaming, tearing clothes and bed clothes	7 mos.	5 mos.	ECT
9	M	M	36	Schizo-phrenia	Suicidal attempt, reticent, said someone was creeping under his skin, destructive, abusive, assaultive, irrelevant remarks, auditory hallucinations, depressed, resistive, insight and judgment impaired, self-absorbed, blocking.	21 yrs.	7½ yrs.	None

* Statistics as of January 15, 1947.
† Treatment of this patient was terminated at Brooklyn State Hospital against the therapist's advice after the psychosis was resolved but before the treatment was completed. The writer does not know the present whereabouts of this patient, but his latest information was that she was well.

TABLE 1—*continued*

Number	"Shock" Treatments			Type and duration of other treatments	Time between "shock" treatments and direct psychoanalysis	Average daily hours of direct psychoanalysis	Duration of direct psychoanalysis	Present length of remission
	Duration	Results						
9 conv. 9 comas	3 wks. 11 wks.	Unimproved Unimproved		Ambul. Insulin 1 mo.	None	2	4 mos.	21 mos.
				Sedation		8	3 days	36 mos.
2 conv. 0 comas	2 mos. 3 mos.	Improved but relapsed		None	7 mos.	2	2 mos.	2 wks.
9 conv. 0 comas	3 wks. 2 mos.	Unimproved Unimproved		Ambul. Insulin 2 mos.	3 mos.	2	3 mos.	34 mos.
0 conv. 0 conv. 3 comas	6½ mos.	Unimproved Unimproved		Ambul. Insulin 1½ mos.	3 mos.	1–3	11 mos.	16 mos.
				None		1	2 wks.	4 wks.
				None		1	5 mos.	25 mos.
0 conv.	3 mos.	Unimproved		Ambul. Insulin 4 mos.	4 mos.	1–3	2 mos.	31 mos.
				None		1½–2	1 mo.	18 mos.

TABLE 1—*continued*

Patient	Sex	Marital status	Age	Diagnosis	Symptomatology	Duration of psychosis	Total hospitalization time	"Shock" Treatments Type
10	F	M	24	Schizophrenia	People following her, auditory hallucinations, especially a whistling sound which represented a code, fear that she was an orphan, depressed, suicidal ideas, suicidal attempt.	7 yrs.	OPD 6 mos.	None
11*	F	S	32	Schizophrenia	Extremely poor contact, inferior conscious control over thought processes, inability to prolong voluntary attention, uncontrolled and delusional thinking, all responses irrational	11 yrs.	11 yrs.	ECT Insulin Metrazol with insulin
12	F	M	23	Schizophrenia	Mutism, stupor, excitement, aggression, viciousness, assaultiveness	5 yrs.	5 yrs.	ECT Insulin Metrazol
13	M	S	27	Schizophrenia	Delusions, hallucinations, terror	2 yrs.	None	None
14	F	M	33	Schizophrenia	Acute anxiety, panic, palpitations, feelings of unreality, insomnia, anorexia, vomiting, weakness, depression	3 yrs.	4 mos.	None
15†	M	S	22	Schizophrenia	Complained that his mind was separating from his body, became excited, placed in restraint, loss of weight, sharp elevation of temperature, talked continually, paid no attention to questions	7 mos.	2 mos.	None
16	M	S	22	Schizophrenia	Delusions, periods of excitement, stupor	3 yrs.	None	None
17	M	S	26	Schizophrenia	Delusions, visual hallucinations, women's faces float in air upside down	9 yrs.	None	None
18	M	M	43	Schizophrenia	Withdrawn, depersonalization	2 yrs.	None	None
19	F	M	52	Schizophrenia	Visual hallucinations, suicidal drive	11 yrs.	None	None

* Patient (11) showed marked impairment of intellectual functioning. resembling organic deterioration.
† Treatment of this patient was terminated at Brooklyn State Hospital against the therapist's advice after the psychosis was resolved but before the treatment was completed. The writer does not know the present whereabouts of this patient, but his latest information was that he was well.

TABLE 1—*continued*

Number	"Shock" Treatments Duration	Results	Type and duration of other treatments	Time between "shock" treatments and direct psychoanalysis	Average daily hours of direct psychoanalysis	Duration of direct psychoanalysis	Present length of remission
			Sedation		4–5	1 mo.	19 mos.
					2	1 mo.	
5 conv. 0 comas	Unknown	Unimproved Unimproved	None	5 yrs.	2–3	7 wks.	2½ mos.
0 conv.		Unimproved					
8 conv. 3 comas 8 conv.	3 wks. 3 mos. 3 wks.	Unimproved Unimproved Unimproved	None	None	1–3	4 mos.	19 mos.
			None		1	10 mos.	39 mos.
			None		2	4 mos.	24 mos.
			Sedation		10	3 days	38 mos.
					3	1 mo. 12 days	
			Yr. Psychoanalysis		1	8 mos.	19 mos.
			Sedation		1	4 mos.	16 mos.
			None		1	3 mos.	7 mos.
			Psychotherapy		2	1 mo.	16 mos.

TABLE 1—*continued*

Patient	Sex	Marital status	Age	Diagnosis	Symptomatology	Duration of psychosis	Total hospitalization time	"Shock" Treatments Type
20	M	S	17	Schizophrenia	Hears voices ordering him to kill his father, jump off the roof and jump under a subway train, depressed, anxious, cries constantly	2 yrs.	2½ mos.	None
21	F	W	33	Schizophrenia	Depression, crying, tremendous anxiety, constant exhaustion, delusions	7 yrs.	9 mos.	None
22	F	S	18	Schizophrenia	Mutism, cerea flexibilitas, wetting, soiling	Unknown	5 mos.	Insulin
23	F	M	33	Schizophrenia	Overactivity, grandiose ideas, incoherent, shifting of mood, bizarre postures, facial grimacing, echolalia, overtalkative, irrelevant, scattered, discordant activity	6 yrs.	3 mos.	None
24	F	S	18	Schizophrenia	Active auditory hallucinations, excitement	9 mos.	9 mos.	ECT
25	F	S	21	Schizophrenia	Delusions, hallucinations, blocking, untidiness, suicide attempt by cutting wrists	3 yrs.	None	ECT
26	F	S	35	Schizophrenia	Anxiety symptoms, fear of fainting, fear of crowds, anxiety attacks	2½ yrs.	6 mos.	None
27	F	M	33	Schizophrenia	Feelings of incompetence and inferiority, little drive or initiative, insomnia, irritability, crying spells, agitated, depressed, suicidal attempt, hazy, confused, paranoid delusions	3 yrs.	6 mos.	None
28	F	M	30	Schizophrenia	Paranoid delusions, incoherent, intense psychomotor activity, mutism, negativism, resistiveness	9 mos.	1 mo.	ECT
29*	M	S	15	Schizophrenia	Moody, retarded, mute, anti-social, felt everything was disintegrating about him, thought he was "dying and evaporating," auditory hallucinations, went into catatonic stupor with negativism, mutism and moderate cerea flexibilitas	12 mos.	17 mos.	Insulin Metrazol

* Treatment of this patient was terminated at Brooklyn State Hospital against the therapist's advice after only three days. Nevertheless, the boy's psychosis was resolved, and he was released from the hospital. He remained out of the hospital for approximately three years, was returned on December 12, 1946, and is still a patient.

TABLE 1—*continued*

Number	"Shock" Treatments		Type and duration of other treatments	Time between "shock" treatments and direct psychoanalysis	Average daily hours of direct psychoanalysis	Duration of direct psychoanalysis	Present length of remission
	Duration	Results					
			None		3–4	2½ mos.	37 mos.
			Psycho-therapy		2	6 mos.	30 mos.
comas d fever	3 mos.	Unimproved	None	None	1–3	1 mo., 20 days	27 mos.
			Psycho-analysis 5 yrs.		1–2	5 wks.	3 wks.
conv.	1½ mos.	Little im-provement	None	4 mos.	1	1 mo.	28 mos.
conv.	2 mos.	Unimproved	Psycho-analysis 6 mos.	1 yr.	1	6 mos.	13 mos.
			None		2	2 mos.	26 mos.
			Psycho-therapy		1	6 mos.	28 mos.
conv.	2 wks.	Unimproved	None	3 wks.	10	2 mos.	12 mos.
					4	7 mos.	
comas conv.	1½ mos.	Some improvement Worse	Thyroid 3 mos.	1 wk.	12	3 days	36 mos.

Table 1—*continued*

Patient	Sex	Marital status	Age	Diagnosis	Symptomatology	Duration of psychosis	Total hospitalization time	"Shock" Treatments Type
30	F	S	19	Schizophrenia	Frightened, confused, feelings of unreality, rich fantasy life, daydreams in color	6 yrs.	OPD	None
31	M	S	30	Schizophrenia	Paranoid trends, hypomania, delusions of grandeur, obscene language, aggressive, assaultive	9 yrs.	15 mos. (Approx.)	ECT
32	M	M	39	Schizophrenia	Overtalkative, religious, discovered philosophy of life, begs for forgiveness, voices talking about him, put his hands in boiling water to boil them	1 mo.	3 wks.	None
33	F	S	26	Schizophrenia	Delusions, hallucinations, suicide attempt with 60 luminal tablets	3 yrs.	2 wks.	None
34	M	S	21	Schizophrenia	Depression, sudden religious fervor, felt he had a personal God, withdrawn, obsessions and compulsions	3 yrs.	None	None
35*	F	M	37	Schizophrenia	Silly, childish, dilapidated, deteriorated, active auditory hallucinations, bizarre delusions, excitement, incoherence, primitive, archaic expressions	2 yrs.	11 mos.	ECT Insulin
36	M	S	21	Schizophrenia	Acute excitement, felt he was somebody else who burned to death in airplane, feared he was going insane, felt his insides were soft and offered no resistance to thoughts penetrating his body	1 mo.	2 days	None
37	M	S	49	Schizophrenia	Auditory hallucinations, "seizures," persecutory delusions	27 yrs.	4 yrs.	ECT Insulin

* This patient referred to in the introduction who had a relapse following a suicide attempt by her sister. The relapse lasted only a few weeks and she is now back at home and free from psychotic symptoms, showing evidence of having gained insight as a result of this pseudo-psychotic experience.

Table 1—*concluded*

Number	"Shock" Treatments Duration	"Shock" Treatments Results	Type and duration of other treatments	Time between "shock" treatments and direct psychoanalysis	Average daily hours of direct psychoanalysis	Duration of direct psychoanalysis	Present length of remission
			None		1	3 mos.	21 mos.
conv.	1 mo.	Unimproved	Hydro. Sedation Vitamins Psychotherapy 5 mos.	1 yr.	1	4 mos.	14 mos.
			None		2	3 wks.	38 mos.
			Psychotherapy		3	3 mos.	21 mos.
			Psychotherapy		1	5 mos.	22 mos.
conv. comas	1½ mos. 2½ mos.	Unimproved Unimproved	None	1 mo. 10 days	5	5 mos.	27 mos.
			Sedation		3	1 mo.	6 wks.
conv. comas	1 mo. 5 mos.	Unimproved		4 yrs.	2	8 mos.	7 mos.

"I had intercourse twice in 11 years. I often tried to go with women, but the voice and my fears prevented it. A long time ago, when I was living home with my mother and suffering with this illness, my sister came home. I heard her say: 'Get undressed. Wash your dick. How do you fuck a whore? I am a whore. I will show you how. I will suck you off.' She was kneeling near the radio and I walked over to her to be sucked off because I'd do anything to get well. She stood up and walked away. I couldn't understand it. When I see a woman, the voice says to her: 'Look out, he is a cop.' And then she turns away." He was asked, *"Why a cop?"* in the hope that somehow it might be explained to him about the hidden wish which has to do with getting women (mother) to turn away from father, i.e., the "cop." He seemed unimpressed and continued: "Hold your breath. Ah! You're a cheap fuck. Why are you smiling now? Swallow! Oh. What a dope. Tell him what you know. Liar! How shall I look? Down. Why don't you do it? Do it." *"Do what?"* "Jerk off. I have been thinking about it a lot. I also told it to that psychologist. He advised me to try it. I can't see it. I want to go out and get a woman. In my thought it comes to me that I can free myself by jerking off. In 1936, I was very sick and had to stay off the job for five months. In those days I went to the whorehouse. It came to me to jerk off, and I fought it. One day I did. The people on the street stopped speaking and laughed as I passed them by. They said out loud, 'He jerked himself off.' I didn't do it since, honest. I had a number of erections." Since he told the physician here what a good boy he was, the physician made much of what a good boy he was. Apparently some transference reaction was taking place in which the physician became identified with his father because the patient continued: "The girls make advances to me. In the park, in my house and at other places. I just walk away from them. I don't bother with them." The implication here being: "I won't disturb your women, father, if you will continue to love me and take care of me."

At about the tenth visit, the physician began to test the consistency of the patient's defenses. Regarding the problem of the voices and the names people called him, the question of validity was raised. R. Z. held steadfast to the concept of this as "thought transference." He mentioned, however, that it was incredible that he should be such a center of attraction. In the last few days he had begun to wonder if his sister was really a whore. He told of an occasion when, acting in his official capacity as a Mason, he was expected to go to a funeral service. As he circled the dead man, he became very hot. When he threw the leaves on the coffin, his hand suddenly became stiff. He heard the nephew of the dead man call public attention to this act. The physician had him associate to this experience as to dream material. "Hot" was "passion" and a "stiff arm," a "stiff prick." Since his associations were so clearly sexual, the meaning of the disguised wish was disclosed to him, and the emphasis was placed on the way forbidden sexual wishes come out under pressure in a disguised form. Some indication of how the unconscious is a reservoir of hidden sexual drives was pointed out to him. This last bit of analysis gave a new kind of super-ego relationship to the ego and resulted in a rush of homosexual memories.

The next time that the patient said: "Hold your breath," the physician told him there was no reason to hold back and that he could tell him his secrets. As if in direct response to this request from the patient's unconscious, the man began: "Do you mean about that woman? It was around 1926. We were on strike. One of the men took me home. These people were friendly with the trainman, who was a fag. We went to a masquerade fairy ball. I was introduced to a woman and we had a box. We looked down at the fairies dancing. I didn't dance with them. After this experience, my sickness got very much worse. Wherever I went in the street, people looked at me and said: 'That is a woman.' No matter where I went, even in other cities, it was the same thing. I never went even to another fairy ball." Once at a doctor's office, he had a rectal examination for hemorrhoids. The rubber finger-cot broke, and he was seized with a pain that went from his rectum over his entire body. (Probably an orgasm.) At another time, while he was in "some kind of a hospital," he received an enema which resulted in the same kind of terrible pain. After this, he found that he couldn't see things. He thought that his eyes were out of focus. Again, he went to a hospital, and they found that his vision was normal.

He went home and found his brother sleeping on the couch. "My brother seemed to say, 'On account of you I got fucked in the ass.' My mother seemed to say, 'Shut up. Don't say these things to him.' A terrible odor suddenly came out of my body. I thought it must come from my armpits. I went to many doctors. They put their noses to my body and they couldn't get that smell. They gave me medicine for it, but it didn't help." PAUSE. "You stink." "Who?" "Me, I guess." *"If you tell a fellow he stinks, what does it mean?"* "He smells bad or he is a bad guy." *"If it happens to be that he is a bad guy, can you smell it?"* "No." This was interpreted to him as the voice of his punishing conscience in relation to the material he had just described. It called him a stinker. *"Now how in the hell could those doctors smell a stinking character?"*

The clarity with which the psychotic recognizes symbols is pointed out as follows: "I go to the restaurant and ask for a piece of cake. They walk away from me. A 'piece' is a 'hump' and 'cake' is eat it. Cock-sucking or cunt-lapping. All food has different meanings. 'They' told it to me. A cruller is a 'prick.' A doughnut is a 'cunt.' Rye bread is an 'ass-hole.' Mustard is 'shit.' When I went past a church or a synagogue, I spit. I did it for a long time, then it came to me, and I stopped." *"What came to you?"* "It was my father. A lot of these things are due to a form." *"What do you mean by a form?"* "Form of insanity." The obvious reason for repressing "insanity" was discussed.

R. Z. blithely continued that many things were due to a form and that he always feared that perhaps he was "insane," but, he continued, he would battle a voice if it told him to do something like "wreck the train." Just before he had quit work as a motorman, he had gotten up to go to work and "was told" to take a shower. While in the shower, he was told that "this day" he would wreck the train. He began to twist in the tub and suddenly tumbled out, falling in such a way as to fracture his wrists. He went to "report sick," and when his story was heard, he was discharged. He was unable to understand this and decided to communicate his difficulties to the F. B. I. He wrote many letters to the F. B. I., but every time he went to mail one, the "seizures" were so terrible that he was unable to do so. He got the idea that he was a psychiatrist and a hypnotist. This thought continued for some weeks during which time he felt he controlled people. When it was determined that this was a reaction-formation against his passivity, i.e., against being controlled, he gave up the delusion.

The patient now perceived a marked increase in his positive feelings toward the physician. He observed that he was getting better and could do anything but telephone. He could write, draw, read a paper, and go out into the street in relative comfort. He missed the analyst over the week-end. In the midst of the session, he suddenly became angry and stated he was going to Yonkers. "You are a son of a bitch. Cock-sucker. Your father put his cock in your mother's mouth, and that is how you were born. I had a feeling stronger than ever to throw myself under an elevated train." (*Analyst*) : "*Father will fuck you in the ass. The train is a big, powerful penis and you wish to lay under it.*" The patient stated that everything had a meaning. "I could never understand it." It seemed that he was beginning to understand something about his homosexual wishes in relation to the physician, but, as yet, no transference interpretation on this score was made. He developed two psychosomatic symptoms as a defense against his mounting anal-attitudes toward the physician: diarrhea and headache. "*This diarrhea is a way of shitting on somebody, isn't it?*" "You know, when I was five years old, I used to sleep with my mother. I would be awakened by my father calling out to her to come into his room. She would go, and I would cry. After a while I would run in to get my mother. I just thought of this." "*No wonder you hate your father. No wonder you hate your mother.*" "But my father was nice to me." "*Then the way to get close to father is to be a woman like mother?*" "When I was very, very young, I guess I must have been a baby, one night I had a condition, and I couldn't get my breath. My father carried me in his arms from room to room and they called the doctor. The doctor put a spoon in my mouth and cured me. The whole story reminds me of cock-sucking. The spoon is a penis." *"I don't see why you call all these things cock-sucking. You're not a homosexual. It seems to me that this is clearly a case in which your life was saved because your father loved you, and the doctor, a man, loved you and saved you. You show a great need to be loved by a man."* "I guess that's a father and son relationship."

The patient was impressed by the physician with the importance of these screen-memories for the purpose of stimulating such memories further. The patient's anger toward the physician mounted in subsequent visits. Each session was: "Fuck yourself. Kiss my ass," and so forth and so forth. He seemed constantly to refer to father taking mother from his bed. His fantasy-life was preoccupied with all kinds of thoughts of intercourse with his sister. During the next few days, he described himself as being hypnotized, and he was compelled to walk on his toes and shake from side to side. He was asked to demonstrate this walk for the physician. It was characteristic of theatrical demonstrations of a "pansy." He felt that crowds of people were following him, jeering at him. *"The interpretation of this may be painful to you, but what it means is that you want to be a woman and you want to attract a man."* "I used to walk for years with my eyes almost shut. When I opened them again, the light actually hurt my eyes. I did it so that I should not see men." *"Did men tempt you?"* "I don't know." *"What about the voice that told you to take men's 'pricks' in your mouth?"* "That came from me. I don't hear that anymore." *"If your eyes were shut you couldn't see yourself either."* "I was ashamed. Tell him you want to suck his cock." *"Who?"* "You. A funny thing happened to me in 1928. The hair fell off my chest and it never came back." The physician examined the patient to verify this psychosomatic compliance. Although his body had more than the usual amount of hair— well distributed—his chest was smooth.

R. Z. began to bring in material which showed more and more his fear and hatred of women. He hated nuns, nurses, and the Christian Science Church, where the parental figure is a woman —Mary Baker Eddy. "When I was 29 and going to whorehouses, I couldn't get an erection. I went to a doctor, and he gave me medicine for it. When the whore got undressed, I began to shake inside. It was a frightening, unpleasant feeling." *"Why do you feel this way about women?"* He could not understand, but the question reminded him of an experience he had once had with a Spanish whore. She undressed, and he failed with her. He asked her to sit on his lap and try it that way. She did and he got an immediate erection. She jumped up and said, "No, not that." "She thought I wanted to put it in her ass-hole." *"Perhaps you did. Why do you think you were able to have an erection?"* He replied promptly, "It's like fucking a man in the ass." *"Sure you didn't see the feared organ of the female?"* This interpretation excited him considerably and pleased him. He felt that he understood so much now.

He recalled a sudden interest in the school for the deaf. After seeing a motion picture of lip reading, he practised it all the way home on the subway. *"Why does this interest you?"* "Cock-sucking." *"Exactly, again using your mouth."* The patient was overjoyed with this new trick of understanding. "Last night it came to me that I had to go to Jersey to shop. I had such conflicts I couldn't buy anything. I went in and out of the store many times. I felt the salesmen were angry with me. Finally I went to a place to eat. I saw a cop and thoughts came to me: crook, pickpocket." (During this recitation, he was visibly agitated.) *"Did you attempt to analyze all this?"* "Sure, cock-sucking." *"How do you arrive at that?"* After some hesitation the patient said, "I don't know." *"Everything isn't cock-sucking."* "Well I used to think of female clothes. I had that thought when I discovered silk or rayon in things I bought. I always wanted to return things, but no store will take things back after you wore them." *"What would you rather be, a crook or a 'fag'?**" "Neither." *"If you had to make a*

* "Faggot"—male homosexual.

choice?" "A crook." *"The cop was your punishing and tempting father. He gave you a feeling of guilt and you hid from yourself the source of the guilt-feeling and accepted a lesser charge. That is why the thought, crook, etc., comes to you about yourself, instead of 'fag.' Why didn't you call me on the telephone when this disturbance was going on?"* "To tell the truth, it wasn't so bad. I didn't have the severe sensations of pain this time."

The following day, the patient proudly announced he had bought a pair of shoes and a shirt. To him, this was an exciting adventure. It was the first clothing he had been able to buy in years. "And you know, the shoes fit. I used to have to buy shoes many sizes too small. I used to go through torture to break in these small shoes. Then I had to get narrow shoes that were open at the toe and heel." *"What does that mean?"* "A cunt." *"You remember how you walked on your toes with your heels lifted. How does that fit in with all this?"* "I was being a woman wearing women's shoes." The material continued to pour out in the same vein, his wish to be a homosexual and his symptomatic action-defenses. When the going got too tough, he invariably experienced a "seizure" and this was being interpreted in terms of super-ego chastisement. He described the "seizure" as a sudden stiffening of the body in various attitudes. The pain he described as pain in the groin, but he pointed to his stomach. He knew where the groin was but forgot when questioned. He suddenly got the thought that he was being punished "for fucking that man's wife." *"Whose wife?"* "Dr. C——'s—that is the way it comes to me." The fear of punishment for intercourse was further introduced to the patient as a more plausible reason for his avoiding intercourse all these years. He was reminded of how he had explained this as not knowing where to find a woman and that if he did, she thought he was a cop, and so forth. As an additional thought, it was suggested: *"I wonder if you ever thought of fucking your mother when you used to sleep with her? What would father have done to you if you had?"* His great struggle now was with his temptation to run away from the analysis. He would have liked to visit his sister in Texas. He went to the Grand Central Terminal every day before his visit to my office, with the intention of buying a ticket to "almost any place" and taking a trip. He had his first dream since he became sick.

Dream: "I was in the kitchen of the house we used to live in. I sat sideways on a chair in front of the window. The shade was drawn. Suddenly I was blind. All was pitch blackness. I struggled fiercely to see. I pulled at my eyes, and suddenly I got my left eye open, and I saw light. I opened the shade to look out and it was cloudy and murky outside. My right eye seemed to stick tight, and the skin on that side of my face got wrinkled tight. Just then my mother and sister came in. I opened the door for them. My mother said, 'Look at what is wrong with your face.' My sister remarked casually, 'Things will be all right again.' "

Associations. "It must be our old apartment." He was unable to talk about the dream. A thought came to him: "I am man and woman. I was able to telephone to you twice over the week-end, but it was very difficult. I visited a friend up-town and the family remarked on how I didn't seem to be 'nervous' any more."

Interpretation. It was pointed out, mostly from the manifest content, that since the analysis, R. Z. saw some light, versus the utter darkness of the not-understanding when he first became sick; his fierce struggle to see was to get the light, to see meanings, and to understand his illness. He fulfilled a wish also to be back with mother and sister.

The following day, the patient arrived in a state of intense excitement. His face was very pale, and perspiration covered his forehead. Instead of sitting down or lying on the couch, he assumed a menacing attitude in front of where the physician was seated. He took a knife from his pocket, released a spring and the blade sprung open. He said that for hours he had been sitting in Grand Central Station planning to run away, but it came to him that he had to go home to get the knife and cut the physician's throat. The physician was not unmindful of the precariousness of his position—but, although prepared to defend himself in the event of any further movement on the part of the patient,

continued a steady barrage of interpretation of a strictly transference nature. *"You want to kill me because I tempt you. Baby
wants to suck my cock. He is hungry. He is frightened. He wants
mother. He wants to destroy father who takes mother away from
him. All you want is love and protection. I will love and protect
you. Put the knife on the desk. Sit down. Lie down. No one will
hurt you."* The physician got up and insisted that the patient
hand him the knife, which he did with obvious relief. For some
time the patient was dizzy, and he began to cry. The physician
consoled him, and at the termination of the interview, he was
informed that the knife would be returned to him tomorrow.

On the following day, when the patient returned, he was again
agitated, but this time his manner seemed to be pleading. All the
belligerence was gone, and he had tears in his eyes. The knife
was placed on the desk, and permission was given to take it if
he wished to. He picked it up and sheepishly put it in his back
pocket. He mumbled something about: "Oh, that, I wouldn't use
it. I just brought it here to show you." On the couch, he again
repeated the thought: "You must go to kill him," meaning the
doctor. He added something about money. The Masons took his
money and Dr. C—— took his money, and "at the Masons,"
they took his money and never explained the ritual. *"How about
wanting to kill me because I took your money?"* "I don't mean
that at all. You gave me protection, power, strength. You explain
things to me." He was able to be aggressive toward the physician
because he found that he could trust him. An interpretation of the
knife-thrust as a gratification of an unconscious sexual wish was
made to the patient. The following day the patient said that he
was happy about the way he felt and that he was optimistic
that better days were coming, in fact, better days were here.

All along in this case, I was expecting some kind of a blow-up,
which seemed indicated, with the defenses constantly being under-
mined through the therapy. With all psychotic patients, positive
and negative transferences are always more intense than with psy-
choneurotics. Failing to gratify the infantile wishes with the
analyst, sooner or later the honeymoon-period terminates, and

dramatic consequences usually follow. Just as the ego prevented R. Z. from wrecking the train, so this same ego prevented him from wrecking the analyst. For this reason, I felt that the risk was not too great in continuing to treat him outside an institution. With each day, the patient showed more and more evidence that he was accepting and adjusting to a world of reality, and the intensity of the symptoms continued to diminish.

The patient asked the physician to go with him to purchase a suit. In the past, he had tried on outlandish clothes that didn't fit, and, even though salesmen argued with him against making such purchases, he nevertheless made them. He was fearful that he might repeat this. He now longed to have friends and to go back to work. The part of him that wanted "to suck a cock" was still there but got weaker. He said that after he left my office "yesterday" and was walking along the street, he suddenly got very dizzy and very nauseated. He said that he just got that feeling again as he was about to come to my office "today." He talked at great length about what a tough neighborhood he was brought up in and how he always had to fight for himself. If he went to his father for help, his father would not help him, but would force him to fight. "I am not a coward. I am not afraid of a beating." "*I believe the reaction you had yesterday and again today was due to my agreeing to help you buy a suit. This is like your father helping you to fight, which would be an expression of love. This intensified your wish to, and fear of, sucking my cock; and the symptomatic response from your stomach stated: I will not accept eating from your penis. I will reject that by vomiting it out. Don't try to make a sissy out of me. I came from a tough neighborhood.*"

The patient admitted that he was excited and happy at the thought that I would go with him to buy a suit, but somehow it all became incorporated in psychotic thought, and he then got the idea that I was only fooling. "Yesterday I went up to the job to ask my friends where I could get a 'hump.' The trouble with me is that I couldn't tell people what I wanted to. Now I can. I am going to make friends. Maybe I can talk on the phone and get a

job. I went to C——'s office today and talked to his secretary.
I asked him to send you the report on my case, and I paid him
$5.00 that I owed him." It was agreed that we would go "tomor-
row" to purchase the suit.

All the next morning, he was nervous, but the actual purchas-
ing of the suit occurred in a perfectly normal manner. As we left
the store, he seemed greatly relieved and called it quite an experience. He was annoyed at his landlady neglecting his room. He
went down and complained to her in a "nice way." She explained
it as "maid-trouble." He didn't want to fight with her because
when he was so very sick, she tried to be nice to him. He had
gone to a show yesterday, and had gotten cramps "like he wanted
to move his bowels." Since this had happened many times before
and proved to be a mental feeling only, he had decided to ignore
it. On the way home, he had to go so badly, he just barely made
his house. He lost the voice and the talking in his head but
expected it to return momentarily. He found it difficult to believe
that normal experiences were real.

"It came to my thought within the past few days that when I
was about two years old, my brother put his cock in my mouth.
My family caught him and from then on, after school he had to
go to the home of relatives until my father came home from
work. I can't be sure if this is a true experience or not, but I
think I can find out. It may be like the thoughts I had about my
sister being a whore. My brother had part of his leg shot away
in the last war. He wears a high shoe and gets along with hardly
a limp. He is not quite all right. If I talk to him about this, he
will begin to cry."

On the following day he stated: "I feel so like a normal person
again today. I took a bath without trouble. It's such a beautiful
day. I sat in the park. What I miss most is a human companion.
Could we go out for a walk?" (The physician agreed.) Outside,
R. Z. felt that the world and people were normal. He continued
to feel "real" during the entire period we were out. He mentioned
that he had had "hot nuts" last night. This thought reminded
him of a fellow he knew who had syphilis. This association was

used to point out to him his fear of a heterosexual relationship because of its castrative threat. He wore his new suit. In many ways, he indicated his great love for his physician, and when this was interpreted to him he said: "In a pig's ass, I love you." This denial was not accepted, but, instead, the concrete evidences of his devotion to the analyst were pointed out to him. He then declared he feared to love any man. If he did (and here he gave an example of a friend who was a stamp collector), he would be inextricably bound to that man—fused, as it were—and it would last forever. This thought was interpreted as homosexual, however well sublimated. As a matter of fact, there was a profound incestuous sexual need in him. A wish again to be fused with mother, in mother's womb, or to be one with mother at mother's breast. This is the basic ultimate goal in any homosexual relationship.

Following this, the patient again began to have thoughts that he was attracting the attention of men. In connection with this, he had thought of the wonderful food his mother fed him—the quantity of it, the quality of it, etc. Because of the sexual nature of the intimacy he craved with his mother, he returned to the homosexual pattern, but this time, not without insight.

Smoking, eating, sleeping, etc., all his thoughts, had a strong sexual significance accompanied by intercourse hallucinations. When asked why, he was unable to explain, although he admitted being aware that all his thoughts led to sex. This hallucinatory experience was pointed out to him as a consequence of his homosexual wishes, which were intolerable, and of his incestuous wishes, which were intolerable, and of his normal genital drives which continued to go ungratified. *"It is essential to the satisfactory conclusion of the case that you permit yourself to seek and obtain a normal sexual outlet."*

R. Z. is now seeking employment and is registered with the United States Employment Service. He has also interviewed a man about a position in his store as a clerk. He called up an old girl friend to make a date, but discovered that she no longer "lived there." He went to the home of a friend—the stamp collector—who arranged with his girl friend to get another girl so that the four could go out. This was the plan for the week-end. The physician informed R. Z. of the date of his own vacation and the patient's voice began to quiver, as if he might cry. He said he didn't understand it, but it gave him "a queer feeling." He went out with his "date" and complained that she was a homely woman. He tried very hard to be sociable, and it gave him a "dull ache." He did some "necking," and the party was out until 6:00 a.m.

R. Z. says that the hair has grown back on his chest during the past three months and it started ever since he got "hot nuts." During the vacation period, he had a good time going to the beaches, to movies, going out on dates, and visiting with friends. He is making some money with a friend in the cigarette business. Only once did he get upset, and this occurred when he made up his mind to go to Lake George to visit the physician. He took the day-liner to Albany; and in Albany he became confused, found himself in a conflict and finally "decided to Hell with it," and took a train and went back to New York City. At the present time, the analysis continues. R. Z. now has no psychotic symptoms and his adjustment is on an increasingly mature level.

Conclusion

R. Z. was presented in person so that the doctors attending the seminar where this paper was read in part could evaluate his present mental health. It was unanimously agreed that he was no longer psychotic. As far as possible, when the patients in the foregoing series appeared to me to be free from psychosis, I had my findings checked by my colleagues. In this way, my opinions regarding the resolution of the psychosis were confirmed.

This leads to the next inevitable question: Will these results withstand the test of time? That question cannot be answered at present; time alone will tell. In the meantime, however, 37 persons, who according to prognoses might face lives of institutionalization, have lived comfortably with society if only for a time. Even if it should be necessary for these patients to return to mental hospitals tomorrow, at least they have been able to enjoy their periods of happiness. Should this prove to be the only gain of my experiment, I would still consider my efforts justified. I hope to report the details of treatment in all of these cases and others as research expands, and also to publish accounts of the progress of the patients listed in the foregoing, in the years to come.

The method of treatment is rather sharply divided into two parts. The first part, the direct psychoanalysis, resolves the psychosis by dealing mostly with that level of mentation which occurs in the pre-verbal period of life and shortly thereafter. The second part is a more orthodox form of psychoanalysis, where the aim is to construct a stable personality and a mature character. The faults in earlier development which are revealed during the study of the psychosis are longitudinally structuralized into later years and, because the patient remembers so much of the psychosis and its meaning, abundant material is obtained that can be utilized subsequently. It is not my intention in this paper to dwell on theoretic concepts; but there is one point on the counter-transference that I believe to be so valid that I shall state it now for the benefit of those who plan to use this method.

The counter-transference is like the attitude of the parent to the child, as distinguished from the transference, which is like the attitude of the child to the parent. The child's ability to disturb the peace of mind of his parent is the earliest known means by which he obtains gratification and protection. When the child is not at rest, it results in the parent feeling unhappily disturbed, and he resents this feeling. Almost in self-defense he attempts to reestablish the former equilibrium. This is constantly recurring in the daily relationship between the parent and the child. The parent is expected to give up his peace of mind again and again to establish peace of mind in the baby. The extent of parental narcissism will determine how much love he can spare for himself for the needs of the child. The immature parent, i.e., the intensely narcissistic one, can withstand only minor assaults and, beyond this, he attacks the annoying little aggressor, thereby establishing an increasingly vicious cycle of attack and counter-attack. Per-

haps this is the earliest source of parental death wishes* against
children. I believe that these unconscious wishes on the part of
the parent are perceived by the unconscious of the child and constitute to him an "unholy peril" with all the accompanying terrifying anxiety thereby provoked. The extent, therefore, of parental narcissism and lack of love for the child as an object must
be an important determinant in the degree to which one is suscep-
tible to schizophrenic reactions. Such a parent is in great need
of love and protection himself and is doubly assaulted by the child
who can love only himself.

In the case of direct psychoanalysis the counter-transference
must be of the nature of the feelings a good parent would have
for a highly disturbed child. The therapist, like the good parent,
must identify with the unhappy child and be so disturbed by the
unhappiness of the child that he himself cannot rest until the
child is again at peace. Then the parent can again be at peace.
If this feeling is present, the patient will *invariably* perceive it
unconsciously. This does not mean that the therapist may not
react automatically to physical attack, but if the basic unconscious
relationship is as described, any conscious reaction on the part
of the therapist will not be misunderstood by the patient as an
alteration of the basically sound interplay of feeling. Schizophrenia, as is well known, is characterized by the most intense
narcissism. The schizophrenic, at the very first interview, makes
it plain that he has no love to spare for his physician, i.e., for
the parental figure. The physician may not understand this help-
less behavior in the patient and may very well respond like an
irate, annoyed parent and proceed to treat the patient with institutionalization, shock therapy and other "riddance" mechanisms.
This is not necessarily a reflection of the extent to which the
physician is narcissistic. If the patient were really an infant, the
physician might quite easily respond with loving care, but what
he sees at this interview is a physically mature adult who only
feels and behaves like an infant. In the beginning then, the physician can expect no more love from a patient than a parent gets

* Be dead—that is quiet or still—in that way I will be let alone.

from a baby. What he gets instead is the patient's total dependency on him.

In order to treat the schizophrenic, the physician must have such a degree of inner security that he is able to function independently, whether he is loved by the patient or not. Or perhaps it would be better to state that the physician must be able to manage with the least possible amount of love from the patient. He must make up for the tremendous deficit of love experienced in the patient's life. Some people have this capacity for loving as a divine gift. But it is possible to acquire this the hard way—by psychoanalysis. It is the *sine qua non* for the application of this method in the treatment of schizophrenia.

It may be well to mention another fact concerning the present adjustments of the writer's recovered patients. The opinion has already been expressed that they have achieved such a degree of integrity and emotional stability and that their character and personality-structures are so well organized that they can withstand at least as much environmental assault as is expected of a normal person. But it should be stressed that in addition to this, they are superior in respect to their amazing understanding of the existence and meaning of the unconscious. I am constantly plagiarizing from their unusual insights in order to understand better some of the bizarre symptomatic actions and symbolic representations of patients I am currently treating. The following examples will explain what is meant.

A patient of mine is the mother of a two-year-old girl. For a period of a week, the child awoke in the middle of the night tearful and frightened. When the mother went to the child, the child told her: "Go away, Mommie. I want Daddy." She made this request of her daddy on each occasion: "Give me my crayon. I want to draw with my crayon." The patient explained to me, "Of course she would have to get it from Daddy. What she really wants is the penis that she feels only Daddy, like God, has the power to give her. After all, who provides things for the various members of the family, except daddy? My husband thought the child was just being perverse and naughty, but I understood immediately that she was aware of the fact that she didn't have a penis, and what she was attempting to do was to remedy this deprivation."

One might think that the patient had read Freud, but what she was doing in reality was to utilize the same source of information that Freud did—the knowledge of the unconscious.

Another example is the paranoid schizophrenic, whom I invited in the latter stages of his treatment to assist me in understanding the peculiar behavior of a catatonic patient. What was puzzling to me was the fact that when the catatonic patient was seated he showed hardly any anxiety. On arising, however, he presented a picture of increasing panic. He seemed to be searching for something. He gazed around the room, looked in his pockets, pulled out his handkerchief, put it back again—all to the tune of increasing distress. I had made many interpretations to the effect that he thought he was castrated and was looking for his penis that had been sacrificed—and so on. None of these proved effective.

It took my paranoid patient to add the ingredient that solved the riddle. He told me:

"He is not worried whether he has a penis or not while he is sitting down because when he is sitting down, he is a girl and that is the way girls do it. [Meaning urination.] When he stands up, he is doing it like a boy, but he is not sure that he is a boy and what he is searching for is the answer to this question."

I felt that if this understanding were valid, my problem was to convince the patient that he was a man, that is, that he had a penis. I tackled it directly at the very next visit. When the patient stood up, I told him to put his hand on his penis and assisted him in this maneuver. As soon as he felt his penis, he was immediately reassured, and the diminution in anxiety was at once apparent. He ceased searching and followed me out of the waiting room with an evident lack of concern. This symptom did not recur.

It seems reasonable to conclude from these experiences that everybody's unconscious perfectly understands everybody else's unconscious, and, whereas most of us cannot command this fund of knowledge in our daily life, it is available to the schizophrenic because of the intimacy in which he lived with it. I hope these remarks will not be construed as an advertisement for schizophrenia because the ringside seats that they have had to the pyrotechnics of the unconscious are hardly compensation for the suffering schizophrenics have experienced.

Many of the writer's patients were treated within the confines of the institutions in which they resided. It was my good fortune to have treated two trained nurses who were schizophrenic patients at the New York State Psychiatric Institute. Because these two former patients now work with me in the treatment of other schizophrenic patients (their insight and understanding of schizophrenia is something amazing to behold and far surpasses mine), I am able to place patients in a controlled environment outside an institution with complete safety. They, with me, assume full responsibility for the protection of the patients and of persons who come in contact with the patients for 24 hours a day, seven days a week. I find that the resolution of the psychosis takes place much more rapidly outside an institution because the amount and character of distractions can be completely controlled.

There are many problems still to be solved: Two are reduction of the enormous amount of time required for this treatment and reduction of its relatively high cost. One must also consider that results, however good, must still be called tentative, and it must be emphasized that no claim of anything whatever is made in this series beyond the evidences supplied by this report.

Discussion *

PAUL FEDERN, M.D.

I am grateful to Dr. Rosen for having shown me his paper and to Dr. Eisenstein for having asked me to discuss it. Although Rosen has been working out his method of psychoanalyzing psychotics for four years, he still gives only preliminary papers. He began his work without knowing about this discussant's experi-

* By participants in a psychoanalytic seminar, New York, N. Y., Nov. 12, 1946.

ences, published in three papers in the 1943 *Psychiatric Quarterly*. Later, he read the papers, and, since then, we had some discussions about his method. The method is a promising and important original contribution. Like every pioneer he carried on his work against a good deal of resistance. However, the Psychiatric Institute gave him the opportunity to continue his way, which seems to be the right one.

I do not know whether it is Rosen's opinion that his cases are cured in the sense of having been freed of the unknown pathologic entity causing schizophrenic or paranoiac psychosis. I myself do not think so. His method consists in attacking by direct psychoanalytical understanding traumatic events of infancy and childhood, and coping with them as being still there, because there is regression to the ego-states of infancy and childhood. Our optimistic viewpoint assumes that this method removes so much of the cause that a satisfactory maturation of the ego catches up with previous failures of development and with gaps in integration. Rosen's good results can be explained—without advancing any new theory—by attributing a great traumatic effect to early sex experiences. Freud assumed such a sexual etiology once in regard to hysteria; later he modified his etiologic theory in regard to the part played by such traumata, yet never abandoned this etiology. Rosen's findings revive this etiologic factor in psychotic cases. However, his cases are freed or relieved of their psychotic states, characterized by a false reality of the psychotic's own making and consequently by badly distorted conceptions of the outside world.

It is common experience that many psychotic cases, by themselves, come back to healthier states, some even to states of health, and some even more quickly under the influence of different organic treatments. We do not yet know the cause and nature of spontaneous improvement.

In contradistinction to spontaneous restoration, with the psychoanalytic treatment by Dr. Rosen, or the analogous but less direct techniques of this discussant, or of Fromm-Reichmann, we know exactly the helping agency that relieves the patients in their regressive states, of fear, of guilt, and of aggression.

The agency is not one but at least two agents—the one is common to all psychotherapy, to all therapy even—it is the *positive transference*. The other is the *participation of the psychiatrist in the psychotic reality of the patient*, when objective reality became unbearable to the patient left alone with his conflicts—which were unconscious during the pre-psychotic period but gained consciousness during the psychotic state.

Rosen uses the positive transference to participate in the patient's psychotic mental life. He not only participates insofar that he accepts their psychotic reality—with all that appears absurd, "nuts," crazy, inconsistent, disintegrated, and moronic to the normal mind. He goes deeper.

His participation is a psychoanalytic one. By means of psychoanalytic understanding, the psychotic reality ceases to be absurd, "nuts," crazy, inconsistent, disintegrated, and moronic for the *normal* mind of the therapist. Through psychoanalytic translation, all the psychotic, *senseless* realities have sense and meaning—not the common-sense meaning of the adult, but the specific sense-meaning of the childhood-state, to which the patient's ego has regressed.

Sometimes Rosen translates a hallucination into its deeper instinctual meaning. In most cases, he uses psychoanalysis directly to recognize what the patient experiences factually. Always, Rosen sincerely accepts the emotional reaction of the patient as adequate to his regressive feelings and helps him directly by explaining to him the feelings which are adequate to the regressive ego-state, in which he has already been living a long period of years. Thus, his technique exactly, and differently, deals with the patient's typical perceptions, conceptions and emotional cathexes; such participation is no easy job.

Rosen's method is in full accordance with this discussant's own assertions in regard to psychoanalysis of psychoses. No free association is used to provoke more unconscious material; the psychotic symptoms and productions are enough material for psychoanalysis. Rosen deals with conflicts and mental pains of the patient and sides with him in his conflicts; he sides with him also in the residues of normal life, when he helps him in shopping and on other occasions.

He deals with the different ego-states with full understanding of the specific conflicts in every *single state*.

It is astonishing that, as far as my knowledge goes, nobody has ever used before the method of *direct psychoanalytic* * approach to the psychotic unconscious products. Even while Jung was convinced that morbid complexes themselves are the toxic agents which create the schizophrenic state, he did not proceed to try to fight the complexes directly.

Sometimes Rosen's method is like a neo-catharsis, when the patient frees himself of his accumulated emotional cathexis by crying, by swearing, by coprolaliac and obscene talking, and even by menacing with death the object of his transference, whose understanding friendship does not give more than that. To a great extent, Rosen is giving belated, but most necessary, sex-education and sex-information to his patients, who are still living in an invisible mental nursery.

It is clear to me that this technique and its good results can only be used by psychiatrists who are as fully convinced of Freud's interpretation of the unconscious as Rosen is. Rosen's findings are also another proof of the truth of Freud's tenets. It may be allowable to compare Federn's (mine) and Rosen's techniques. Federn interprets the psychosis in the sense of Freud, for one's own better understanding, and then uses one's understanding to make the patient slowly understand himself better and face his own problems with the healthy part of his ego, then slowly to restore more and more health to the ego. Furthermore, Federn's method is focussed on re-repression.

Rosen's method is a direct fighting of the unconscious that became conscious, without caring much about its re-repression. To use this method is possible when the patient's ego is still, to a great

* Dr. Rosen wishes at this point to express his gratitude and appreciation to Dr. Federn for having coined the phrase "direct psychoanalysis" to describe Dr. Rosen's method of treatment.

part, healthy and able to cooperate with the psychoanalyst. It appears, however, that many more cases can be approached by his direct psychoanalysis than we may assume.

We should not forget that psychotics come to the psychiatrist in a state made worse by the necessity of defending their psychotic reality against a host of normal persons, who do not believe the patient's reality. And the normal part of the patient's ego cannot side either with the psychotic part or with the normal persons. Therefore, the healthy part usually soon loses all strength and reacts with all kinds of complicating neurotic behavior, especially with anxiety states and obsessions. The security of being understood by the psychiatrist, by the nurse, and by other people, allows the normal part of the ego to regain its strength.

To understand the psychotic, one must fully understand the unconscious. I pay my tribute to Dr. Rosen that, as a psychiatrist, he has incorporated Freud's work into his own mind, with great clarity combined with pioneer enthusiasm; I also pay tribute to the therapeutic methodologic progress. Most cases will need further watch and social help. Records will be checked by other workers. Such checking presupposes the same understanding of the unconscious which Rosen attained by reading Freud.

For this reason, I venture a word of caution concerning too wide experimentation with this treatment. It was devised as a last resort to save the life of a boy dying of exhaustion in a state of acute catatonic excitement—a situation where any effort whatever would have been warranted. Justification of this treatment in other cases has so far been mostly empiric. It may have dangers which have not yet been recognized. Since danger to life would require recognition by the physician, and since the therapy as a whole is based on psychoanalysis, I suggest that for the present it might be well to confine experimentation with it to trained psychiatrists who are also fully qualified psychoanalysts. It may be safe for the psychiatrist who has not been analyzed to attempt use of this method, but it would be well to make certain of this before extending its scope.

PAUL HOCH, M.D.

I think that Dr. Rosen's paper and his previous paper which was published in the *Psychiatric Quarterly* bring up a number of questions which we will have to discuss. First, are some of the points which he raises as to the therapy of schizophrenia in general.

The textbooks which deal with schizophrenia usually start out with the statement that the treatment of schizophrenia is impossible because a schizophrenic patient is unable to form any sort of transference relation with the physician; therefore, any form of psychoanalytic therapy with a patient is not feasible. A great number of psychiatrists before Rosen voiced the opinion that this idea was wrong. The case which he presented this evening also demonstrates that the patient is able to form a transference relationship with the therapist. However, this transference is a very weak one, a very precarious one. If you go back to the childhood relationship of the schizophrenic patient, you will find one thing which is maintained practically all his life, namely, a sole—I would say restricted or monopolistic—emotional relationship to one or another member of the family which later on is probably transferred to one person who pays attention to him. This relationship, however, has a very narrow base. The patient is unable to broaden the base and branch out to form other emotional attachments. Nevertheless he has developed a firm attachment with one or the other parent and this attachment can be used to some extent for therapy.

Another point in the transference situation, Dr. Rosen indicated in his paper quite clearly, especially when the patient started to threaten him, that this transference relationship with the therapist is a very precarious one, a very ambivalent one. The analytic relationship which characterizes the schizophrenic rather than the neurotic patient is based on a simultaneous love-hate relationship. The patient suddenly can break up the transference or turn around and threaten, or even kill, the therapist. Ferenczi and others, who used a method very similar to Dr. Rosen's, were on several occasions threatened by their patients, and there were some

who even paid the penalty for not taking into consideration the
ambivalent transference-relationship of the patient. But all this
shows that it really is possible to form a transference relationship
with the patient, even though this transference relationship is only
maintained for a while.

Until now, it has been impossible to cure the majority of schizophrenics with any method, organic or psychoanalytic. A great
many therapies which have been used in the treatment of schizophrenia have not lasted more than five years. No therapy for the
treatment of schizophrenia has survived this five-year followup.
I hope that Dr. Rosen's will survive this time span.

I should like to take up another issue which is constantly confused: the concept of deterioration. This term is very loosely used
and many patients are judged deteriorated who are not. Symptoms
of regression are usually interpreted as signs of deterioration, and
no therapy is given. I emphasize that a great many patients who
appear to be deteriorated are not deteriorated. Schizophrenic regression is different from deterioration. In regression, the patient's
ability to make contact remains, although he is unable to use it.
The patient can bounce back again to some degree from any type
of regression. Nevertheless, if we are dealing with a patient who
is truly deteriorated, it is clear that the therapy will be very difficult. I cannot accept the case presented by Dr. Rosen as deteriorated because a fully deteriorated patient would not have established transference in 10 sessions as well as this patient did and
verbalize his difficulties as well as this patient did. I am sure that
this patient showed only signs of regression, but was actually not
deteriorated and that, therefore, contact was possible.

Dr. Rosen mentioned in his paper, as is also mentioned in the
literature of psychoanalysis, that the treatment of the schizophrenic should actually be a treatment of his ego. This concept
assumes that in schizophrenia a very strong ego regression is
present, and, if we are able to support the ego, we may be able
to lift the patient out of the psychosis. The therapy aims at
strengthening the ego which is weak. It is obvious today that
schizophrenia is not alone an impairment of the ego, but is an

impairment of all three layers of the psyche (Freudian interpretation of the psychic organization). The patient not only shows a weak ego, but a weak super-ego which goes down very fast during the psychosis. The id is also impaired, and the interrelation of the three layers is badly coordinated. Because all three layers are affected, the treatment of such patients is very difficult and in many cases unsuccessful.

Schizophrenia can be treated with many methods, and all these methods until now have demonstrated one thing: that if you employ a continuous drip method containing affection and protection, the patient is able to lift out from the psychotic state to some extent and is able to function. But very few patients, if you follow up their cases for a number of years, are capable of maintaining this form of recovery against everyday stress when the treatment is discontinued. Here my skepticism comes in, because until several years have elapsed after the termination of treatment, I am not prepared to accept this patient as cured. These patients are functioning better, are lifted out of psychotic states, but the underlying structure on which the psychosis grows is maintained.

No therapy known today will alter the basic structure. All therapies have until now accomplished just one thing: They have reduced the emotional pitch which is behind the symptoms of the patient and reduced the marked anxiety which is present in many patients. I had the privilege several years ago of discussing the paper of Dr. Schilder, who originally expressed the opinion that if we are able to limit this great panic, this great anxiety in the schizophrenic patient, which, he surmised, is probably based on catastrophic infantile experiences, we would be able to cure the patient. He experimented with psychotherapeutic methods, and he even treated some with group therapy. This lasted a few years, and then he said: "The improvements are mostly only temporary. Today I am more inclined to believe schizophrenia is an organic psychosis." In other words, his ability to make permanent cures was very meager. These "cured" patients, under some stress from an unexpected quarter, very suddenly relapsed. One of the interesting things to watch in schizophrenia is how a supposedly cured patient under stress of some sort suddenly blossoms out full-fledged with the previous symptoms. How is it possible that in a few days the patient is again back in the same state when we believed him cured?

Another point: In a large number of schizophrenic patients, acute and chronic, the disorder is oscillating and cyclical. If this is not taken into consideration, therapeutic results can be obtained which are bound to the cycle of the patient, but not actually to the therapy. Psychotherapy, psychoanalysis, homeopathic methods, "shock" treatments—I could name 15 other methods, all of which effect temporary cures.

We have to be cautious in appraising Dr. Rosen's method, but I am glad he has the optimism to experiment with this kind of treatment. We shall have to approach his method with the necessary caution and with the necessary criticism. The treatment of schizophrenia is full of claims of cure, with claims of recovery, and if we look into these claims, we see a temporary reduction of anxiety, a temporary meeting of stress situations, but the individual's immunity to stress and to emotional upheavals is very low, and it usually remains, even after treatment, rather brittle.

JULE EISENBUD, M.D.

I have no prepared discussion; nevertheless, I should like to comment on the paper and on one or two of the points raised by Dr. Hoch.

We have witnessed a rather remarkable case presentation this evening, and we ought to evaluate it very carefully and be very careful not to lump it in with other statistics which have been referred to. I don't want to quibble on the question of whether or not this patient began therapy in a deteriorated state or whether his cure, if it is a cure, will last five years. (Why we set a date of five years in any case, we don't know. It is a rather arbitrary figure. It is questionable whether life can guarantee five years of stability to any person.) What we have seen, however, whether or not this patient was deteriorated when he began, whether or not his cure will last, is that he made the beginnings of a remarkable recovery under purely psychologic auspices. I don't feel quite right in comparing this method to homeopathic methods or frontal lobotomy or "shock." This is a purely psychologic method.

If we try to dissect what we have heard and assay the therapeutic factor from the welter of material, it is apparent that we are going to run into difficulty, and it was apparent to no one more quickly than to Dr. Rosen, who began by stating that many factors are still obscure. At the outset, however, I don't think that we have the right even to consider the question of spontaneous remission in this case. The man had been ill for 27 years; if he started to become well at the time the physician began to handle him, I am prepared to agree that there is a connection, regardless of what may be said about a schizophrenic cycle.

Now, what does Dr. Rosen do? Speak directly to the unconscious? It is questionable whether anyone can speak directly to the unconscious, but we know what he means. I am prepared to hazard that Dr. Rosen speaks to a person, not to an unconscious— a person who has an unconscious, perhaps, but whose unconscious is, nevertheless, bounded by some sort of an ego, however rudimentary. When Rosen says he speaks directly to the unconscious, we know what he means. He gets right in with direct interpretation. He recognizes undoubtedly that he is dealing with a disturbed ego. He treats the patient as if the early traumata, the early ghosts, were still present and on the scene. Time has no meaning. He feels that, as Dr. Federn said, this patient is still in an invisible nursery. There are a number of interpretations which he has read you which one could quibble about. It looks very easy, just as it looks easy when Tilden plays tennis! Everything goes in the right place. We can't question whether the interpretations were absolutely correct; we don't know. There's one thing, however, which has impressed me about the work of Dr. Rosen during the time that I have been privileged to observe it, and that is the fact that, so far as I can observe, Dr. Rosen has absolutely no hostility toward the patient, toward the psychotic patient. This, I think, is a very important factor.

If we read the papers of Frieda Fromm-Reichmann, for instance, we get the impression that the transference, in the case of the psychotic, is a very exquisite, delicately balanced affair, for the slightest misstep on the part of the physician will result in catastrophe in the therapy. I believe that this is the case, not only because of the ambivalence of the patient, but because of the ambivalence of the physician, where a physician has to be watching at every moment to see that—because of the unfortunate effects—he doesn't slam the door in the patient's face or interrupt the patient to answer a phone call. Such a treatment will be dangerous at every moment.

I have observed Dr. Rosen with several of his patients, and at first I was astounded to notice the casual way in which he just threw overboard the exquisite instruction of Frieda Fromm-Reichmann. I watched, and I watched, and I said to myself, that *I* could never treat a patient with such a casual attitude. But I noticed one thing, that as far as I could observe, Rosen is not afraid to do this because he has no hostility toward the patient whatsoever. The average physician prefers not to treat psychotics to start with. If he does, he feels safe in having his own ego between him and the psychotic process, and safe if he has a good hunk of the patient's ego between the two participating parties.

Rosen isn't afraid of mixing right up with the patient, isn't afraid of being engulfed by the process. He is not afraid of the seductive lure of the world of fantasy to which psychotic individuals cling, nor is he afraid, apparently, of the extreme dependency of the psychotic which at times can be vicious and which most of us regard as an unwanted burden. I think it is these factors which are, as much as anything I can observe, responsible for the excellent results which Dr. Rosen gets.

I think many of us could make interpretations almost as good as Dr. Rosen has given, if we really believed in the unconscious. (Many of us don't.) But I don't believe that there are many people who could approach the psychotic with the complete absence of fear, the complete absence of hostility, the identification without the need to shuttle back and forth frequently to a safety zone, that characterizes Dr. Rosen's approach. And for these reasons,

I wonder whether Dr. Rosen's method will ultimately turn out to be generally applicable. However, we have lots of time before us.

Other people will try this method, and Rosen himself will unquestionably see the five-year mark and give us statistics. Whether or not the transference can be resolved so that the strength that he is able to infuse into these people will take as a permanent graft, and whether he will be able firmly to cement the building blocks of reality into these regressive egos, we don't know. But we shall see.

MELITTA SCHMIDEBERG, M.D.

I agree with Dr. Eisenbud's remarks, in particular those concerning the counter-transference. This is important in every treatment, but especially so with patients beyond the pale of ordinary society, such as psychotics and criminals.

I have achieved full cure with two patients, a boy of 16 suffering from paranoid dementia and a schizophrenic man of 23, both of whom were followed up for a period of nine years. Both fell in love, married happily, and were able to handle difficult situations. I followed up the improvement in a schizophrenic defective woman patient of 28 for 14 years. She managed her life successfully and without relapse, though she probably still had some delusions. I achieved an I.Q. of 100 in a schizophrenic defective child of 3½ who could not talk nor do anything when she came to me. On the other hand, I had two cases which did not show improvement. I have treated 25 schizophrenic, schizophrenic-defective or dementia paranoid cases, and one of true paranoia, achieving varying degrees of improvement. One patient with dementia paranoides showed improvement after eight interviews, and I followed him up for two years. I achieved a good improvement in a schizophrenic woman of 60 who had been in institutions a number of times. I treated only those patients who were not too disturbed to be seen at my office. One had been certified; several were certifiable, and some had had "shock" treatment without results.

Dr. Rosen is to be admired for achieving results in 37 out of

38 cases, a record better than my own. It is possible that it is easier to bring about improvement in the worst cases because they do not have the normal defenses. My technique differs slightly from Dr. Rosen's—I do not wait for the patient's free associations, but interpret whatever material I get. I analyze delusions, hearing of voices, etc., just as I do a neurotic symptom. I try above all to analyze the aggression and anxiety, and constantly watch the transference. It is very unstable and likely to change from moment to moment because of intense anxiety and ambivalence, but if the patient receives relief and sympathy, he becomes more attached than any other patient. He clings to the analyst as a protection against his overwhelming anxiety, regarding the analyst as his last contact with reality.

JOSEPH MEIERS, M.D.

I have taken the liberty to insert myself into this discussion, in spite of the little time left, only because I think I may be able to contribute a bit from the point of view that is of interest today, in the public eye, more than anything else—mainly the potential gain from Dr. Rosen's procedure, to a better possibility of coping with the more chronic manifestations of mental illness (psychoses) as we have them in an overwhelming majority in the state and other large public mental hospitals—a fact which is, as you all know, of such paramount concern both from a purely psychiatric viewpoint and, at the same time, also from the vantage point of national health. And it so happens that, after all, Dr. Rosen *did* obtain his primary incentive and idea for his present endeavor while working in a large state hospital. . . .

Thus he will agree with me, I think, if I say that he could be easily supplied with a couple of hundred, or even thousands of carefully selected—what he would call "deteriorated"—cases of various types of schizophrenia in order to try his method, as described here today, on them with all possible controls and variations. Right now, I recall a case of a young girl who had been in the hospital (one where I worked) from 11 to 16½ years of age. I started to try the method of "direct approach" and

actional-interpretive dialogue with her, with a modicum of success. I had not then read of Rosen's procedure and was depart-
ing from somewhat different bases, largely those of the psychodramatic method . . . I cannot now go into the details of that
case and its tentative management. I have mentioned it *merely*
to underscore that the case of this young girl had become, after a
short series of electric shock treatments, completely "inactivated"
as to treatment. She was moderately catatonic, grabbed her own
and other patients' food, was most of the time in a camisole,
inert, indifferent apparently. In short, she was what not only Dr.
Rosen here tonight, but most colleagues might consider as
"typically deteriorated." You will forgive me, if I want to make
it *a point* that we must, for very important reasons, *differentiate*
between a really "deteriorated" and a merely "inveterated" case.

True mental deterioration is, of course, as all of you know, not
hard to establish when we see it in senility, certain forms of alcoholism, etc. On the other hand, one often is induced to assume
"deterioration" falsely—mostly in certain forms of catatonics,
and mixed catatonic-paranoids, where a thorough testing is near-
to-impossible because of the patient's inaccessibility.* To refer to
the case of my unfortunate child patient once more—while she
seemed to nurses and others for all practical purposes, somewhat
of a living "mummy," a few shots well aimed at her ego, revealed
that she not only was able to write (after five years of well-nigh
complete inactivity!) but that she also recalled memories of her
puberty and before. Thus, I hope to have your agreement, to some
extent, at least, when I say that it is crucial—just from the viewpoint of selecting cases for the "Rosen method"—to avoid carefully the real "mentally deteriorated," inasmuch as they would
unnecessarily tip the scales of the results.

However, it is essential to stress the features of "inveteration,"
i.e., of sheer *long duration* of a psychosis (and even neurosis) on
the psyche of the patient as such—a point that is not too often
brought to our attention. There seems to me—if you permit a
very sketchy hint—to be these *two* principal sides in inveteration:

* Roe, A., and Shakow, D.: Intelligence in Mental Illness. New York Acad-
emy of Sciences. New York. 1940.

1. The patient, whether hospitalized or extramural, is more and more put on his defensive and thus develops an ever-thickening maze of both intra-psychic and inter-personal defenses.   2. All the sum total of his thoughts, convictions (and errors!) about his environment and himself, his illness, etc., becomes almost impermeable. *None* of us, whether psychotic, neurotic, or "normal," wants to be *"all wrong"* in his judgments, recollections, and conclusions. Thus, we observe so often a persistence of "delusional" material from the past, where there is no actual delusional thinking at present. These two features, interlocked, tend to form (in the "inveterated" case much more than the fresh one) the almost cretaceous *"crust of inveteration"* which is superadded to the original "core" of the psychotic trauma and its constitutional matrix. It is this which we are up against in dealing with inveteration—even without factual "deterioration."

In regard to this problem, I think three discussional approaches we heard here tonight were most remarkable. As for Dr. Paul Federn's contribution—to which I largely agree in its evaluation of Dr. Rosen's work—I am sure had he been here in person, he might have participated in the discussion of the "deterioration" ("inveteration") problem, too. As it is, I think we all are deeply grateful for what he has given in his message to the discussion.

On the other hand, I feel that Dr. Hoch's cautious approach is fully warranted. Even so, he did *not* seem to deny, even from the official viewpoint—as it were—of the New York Psychiatric Institute, of which we may consider him factually, if not formally representative, that Dr. Rosen's method of "direct [and as I would add, 'inter-actional'!] approach" is worth being tried out further, final judgment being reserved for a duration of a few years of maintained cures.

Now, as to that "time limit" of *five* years—arbitrary as it may seem, some line of duration has to be chosen! How happy would all of us be, including Dr. Hoch and all the state authorities, if the curative results in Dr. Rosen's cases prove to last even slightly less than five years. May I point out, by the way, that these *five* years have an important practical significance, as the law stands, from the point of view of the "established" duration of the "incurable mental illness" case, as it comes up in marriage annulment, etc., law suits. The consequences that would ensue from cures of "inveterated" psychoses *after* they had been declared "incurable"—well, we need not go into that here and now.

The important question—and one which will have to be scrutinized carefully in subsequent investigations—is the following: How much of the curative result in Rosen's cases is due entirely to the "purely" and typically psychoanalytic-interpretive approach, no matter how much widened and extended beyond the customary boundaries of the classic method? How much, on the other hand, is due to that inter-actional, "dramatic" element, of the "living together," as it were, of therapist and patient through mutual experiences, as described tonight by Rosen and earlier in his article in the *Psychiatric Quarterly* of April 1946? On the basis of my own experiences I am greatly inclined to attribute a lion's share to the inter-actional, "dramatic" nature of the approach.* An authority in orthodox analysis, like Kubie, warns against the "direct interpretation" or confrontation of the patient with results of free association *not* understood by the patient himself— in typical psychoanalysis, as this often leads to embarrassing results, if not worse.† Nothing like that can be observed in true psychodramatic, inter-actional work with the patient—for the simple reason, as it appears, that it is the patient, and only he, who does the interpretation that affects him and that he "acts out" the emotions connected with, or brought up by, that "interpretation."

HYMAN SPOTNITZ, M.D.

About seven years ago I became interested in treating a series of post-psychotic patients who had previously been hospitalized for their psychoses. After I had treated them for a while, I became impressed with the same factors and had the same type of feeling that Dr. Rosen has summarized tonight with the words, "talking directly to the unconscious." About three years ago, I

---

* Meiers, Joseph L.: Origins and Development of Group Psychotherapy. Beacon House. New York. 1946.

† Kubie, Lawrence S.: The Nature of Psychotherapy. Bull. N. Y. Acad. Med., 1943.

stopped most of my work in this field. However, I am glad to be able to confirm that this experience actually did exist for me, too. It is possible to feel as if one is talking to the unconscious of the patient. Patients sense the feeling of communion with them and immediately begin to respond, and the material, which is readily interpreted, leads to a rapid amelioration of symptoms over a period of weeks or months.

My last work of this type was done at a local hospital with a case of ulcerative colitis. The patient was referred to me for psychoanalytic therapy, because a gastro-enterologist considered that he was on his deathbed and would have to have an operation immediately or die within a few days. The psychiatric service wanted to demonstrate what could be done with psychotherapy. I "spoke directly to his unconscious," that is, whatever he said was immediately interpreted with what appeared to me to be its symbolic meaning. This patient walked out of the hospital within three weeks with a dramatic improvement. I had at that time known and predicted that he would relapse. The feeling I had was that his improvement was due to the pain he was experiencing and his desire to escape from rapid-fire interpretations. He later did have a partial relapse and was treated subsequently along more standard analytical lines. He has now been symptom-free for a year and a half.

I want to compliment Dr. Rosen on his courage and on his deep insight in this field. I feel it requires a great deal of courage, devotion, and sincerity to do this type of work.

Editorial Comment *

Oh perish the use of the four-letter words
Whose meanings are never obscure;
The Angles and Saxons, those bawdy old birds,
Were vulgar, obscene and impure.
But cherish the use of the weaseling phrase
That never says quite what you mean.
You had better be known for your hypocrite ways
Than vulgar, impure and obscene.†

* Reprinted from Psychiat. Quart. 21:117–119, 1947.
† From "Ode to the Four-Letter Word." Anonymous?

The "vulgar, impure and obscene" words which English has inherited from the Angles and the Saxons loom large in the vocabularies of psychotic patients. But when an investigator and earnest student attempts to rescue a deteriorated patient sunk in the morass of catatonic stupor by interpreting his delusions and hallucinations and speaking to him in the same infantile words flung at him by accusing voices—thus to draw out his mental content, to be understood, and to gain a response—he must watch his step or he will be misunderstood by the uninformed and suspected of evilmindedness. The editor has asked patients at discharge conferences (staff meetings) to repeat the exact words heard by them, words which the patient had just described as unreal or imaginary "voices." Rarely can a patient be induced to do so. Often he excuses himself by saying he "cannot remember" but sometimes by frankly saying: "Oh no! There are ladies present."

The unconscious, when coming to verbal expression, does not choose the "weaseling phrase" but the hearty Anglo-Saxon words which mean just what they say. Every experienced psychiatrist has heard from the lips of patients known to come from homes of culture and refinement, torrents of vulgarity and obscenity when in a maniacal rage. One is prompted to exclaim: "Where *could* she have learned such words!" And the deteriorated hebephrenic or catatonic—without the spur of rage or excitement, without any appearance of shame—uses words and phrases that so shock the prudish that interns and nurses have asked to be excused from service on certain wards.

The editor and his associates feel that a keen sense of clinical duty makes it imperative upon them to quote—when quotations are essential to an unbiased presentation of clinical material—patients' and therapists' remarks exactly as they are made. An attempt to "purify" the clinical record by substituting parlor or scientific phraseology of the twentieth century for four-letter words known to everyone would be a species of prudish hypocrisy unworthy of a medical publication. The members of the editorial staff are not addicted to the employment of scatology in their own conversation. They regret that prudes may find on the pages of the *Quarterly* words employed—when essential to the context—that may give offense to the Miss Nancies of both sexes, but the regret is wholly for the state of mind of such prudes, and there is no intention whatever of modifying the editorial policy of truthfulness to details in quotations.

We submit here and now that psychiatry is a profession for adults and that it is time for psychiatrists in general to act adult. It is not a profession for the sort of lady, male or female, who shudders at four-letter words and the mental images they invoke.

These remarks are occasioned by the fact that in this issue of the *Psychiatric Quarterly* we are publishing the second report on the successful treatment of psychotics by a method which is purely psychotherapeutic. This report summarizes the results of treatment in 37 successfully-treated cases, but it is for the most part a clinical record of a single patient, a man who had had schizophrenia for 27 years, who had been treated four years in an institution, had received insulin therapy (60 comas) and electric shocks (20 convulsions) and had remained unimproved for four years thereafter, prior to the institution of direct analytic therapy.

Certain recognized psychiatric procedures are horrifying to persons who hear of them for the first time: "Shock" treatment may be interpreted as cruelty, and the reaction it brings on may be terrifying to the inexperienced onlooker. The coma of insulin "shock" resembles death; the convulsions caused by metrazol and electric shock may cause bone fractures. Yet the public in general and the next of kin of hospital patients have come to accept the presumed risk of injury or possible death when it is understood that apparent cures are often effected by these methods: indeed, relatives now often demand that "shock" treatments be used.

Treatment by direct analytic therapy will be as horrifying to some persons who hear of it for the first time as treatment by the shock therapies is, for direct analytic treatment is planned to meet psychotic patients on their own level—a very regressed level. All severe mental disorders involve regression, in one form or another, to early childhood or even infancy, regression in the way of individual acts or reactions in the neuroses and in a whole altered state of life and consciousness in the psychoses. This is particularly true in dementia præcox. We all know what the deteriorated schizophrenic may occasionally say or do. To point out the A, B, C's of psychiatry—he often speaks of things in the "dirty words" which a child would use in a tantrum. It is sometimes necessary, if one is to meet the regressed schizophrenic on his own level, to employ words he hears in his hallucinations. These may comprise the only vocabulary that will make an emotional contact with his distraught self-absorption and gain a response.

All of us know what those words are. Most of us learned them as children. All of us have seen them in public or school toilets. Anybody so squeamish as to shudder at them or at the desires or actions toward which they point has no business in psychiatry and psychotherapy.

Throughout modern times the lot of the medical man, whenever sex "has reared its ugly head," has not been a happy one. The practice of obstetrics was hampered from the time the physician replaced the midwife and the bed the obstetrical chair, so that a sheet could be drawn to cover the genitalia of some high-placed lady during the business of birth. The first gynecologists, as witness the case of Dr. Marion Sims, were objects of intense suspicion, dislike, and opprobrium. They were whispered about by the general public, denounced from the pulpit and by colleagues in the medical profession. Nobody in modern psychiatric work has forgotten the persecution and the vilification endured by Freud when he began his researches into the rôle of the sex instinct.

We think psychiatry should have attained at least near-adulthood by this time. It is somehow astonishing to see a modern psychiatrist reacting as a mental hospital chaplain did recently in discussing "Freudian filth."

We are quoting, without the author's permission (for we have no idea who the author is) from the same bawdy little poem, "Ode to the Four-Letter Word," with which we commenced this discussion:

Let your morals be loose as an alderman's vest
If your language is always obscure.
Today, not the act, but the word is the test
Of vulgar, obscene and impure.

Note—1952

Such patients as I have described in this paper are not supposed to remain well beyond a hypothetical five year period. That period has now passed almost twice. Some of the patients, after analysis, married and had children. Others took jobs or started businesses of their own. One of them, after concluding his pre-medical training, was admitted to medical school and is now in his sophomore year. Seven of these patients have taken on the custodial care of one or more of my other psychotic patients.

Six patients in this series, who are described under numbers 11, 15, 22, 25, 29, and 33, are presently psychotic and probably institutionalized. Of these, patients 11, 15, 22, and 29 were discharged from the hospital after resolution of the psychosis but without analysis. Patient 25 was in the midst of her analysis when the parents interrupted treatment under the influence of colleagues who insisted that she should have insulin and electric shock therapy combined, and that the longer the parents delayed giving her that kind of treatment, the more hopeless her case would become. The last word we had on this patient was obtained from her parents in 1951, and it was to the effect that she was receiving custodial care in a private psychiatric hospital; the shock treatment had been administered. Patient 33, also in the midst of the analytic part of her therapy, became violently hostile to me. She gave expression to many latent paranoid ideas and began "acting out" both at home and on the street. The father interrupted treatment without my consent and took her to a state hospital where, against my advice, shock therapy was inaugurated. When this failed, psychosurgery was performed and at the present time I have learned, from a former resident at the hospital where she was then treated, that she is severely regressed and has been discharged after a period of observation to another state hospital where she receives maintenance shock treatments and custodial care.

Up to my latest information, the other 31 patients in this series are not now psychotic and are doing well. Those who received a full analysis after the resolution of the psychosis are doing particularly well; these include patients mentioned in the first paragraph of this note.

The Perverse Mother

A SCHIZOPHRENIC is always one who is reared by a woman who suffers from a perversion of the maternal instinct. In this paper I will try to present the material that over the years focused my attention on this hypothesis.

First, we have observed that without exception, every psychotic patient we have had has passed through a phase of his illness which was characterized by a preponderance of paranoid ideas. Many patients remain at this stage which the colleagues agree to call paranoid; some go on for one reason or another to levels of deeper regression, namely hebephrenia and catatonia, and others even improve back to a severe form of neurosis, particularly of the obsessive, compulsive type. Even though a patient is first seen by us in a mute catatonic phase of the psychosis, the hospital record, if carefully made, will indicate that the patient went through a paranoid period where the complaints were essentially, "I am followed by the FBI," "Somebody is after me," "The governor or the president should be notified," (sometimes the landlord or the local police), but in any event it is clearly indicated that somebody hates the patient and he needs protection. It is noteworthy that I can recall no instance where the manifest protector was a woman. Sometimes the paranoid idea is expressed as hatred against the official but never because of anything the official did against him; rather it is always because of something the official failed to do to protect him.

I am reminded of a patient, a mute catatonic, who did not speak to me for the better part of a year, whose pre-catatonic anamnesis included the following story told by her husband: "My

wife had been depressed and unhappy and sleepless for a number
of weeks. I found out later that she believed her father had tried
to kill her mother. One of the doctors consulted suggested we go
to a hotel in the mountains. While there, my wife ran into the
corridor one night screaming that I wanted to kill her, and it was
only with great difficulty that she could be calmed down." This
is an example of the kind of threatening material we find in the
case histories of mute patients.

In other cases, I see the patients in just the phase of the illness
where paranoia is so marked. Very often, in addition to other
evidences of being hurt, the patient fears that the medicine or
sedative is poison, that the food has been tampered with, or that
it smells and tastes odd, and in some instances the mother or the
cook who served the patient is violently assaulted as being responsible for the food arriving in such a condition. Again, the
patient goes through all kinds of magical maneuvers, having for
their object such a combination or sequence of the food, or such
a ritual in eating it, that he will not be poisoned.

Without being able to clearly formulate the thought, for a
number of years I had the feeling that this phase of the illness
was absolutely meaningful and important and somehow contained the clue to the patient's distress. Not one iota of conscious
truth existed in any of the patient's delusions, and yet he held to
every detail of them with such an intensity of conviction and
such affect that I felt in the background some unconscious idea
I had to understand.

Until a year ago, I toyed with all sorts of possible explanations.
To mention only a few: the unresolved oedipal conflict, the death
of one or both parents, incestuous experience at an early age,
excessive masturbation, fellatio, homosexual passivity as a de-
fence against incest, coprophagia, etc. The nature of the material
elicited from patients failed to sustain these considerations as
being prime etiologic factors. They are solely consequences of the
prime factor. I was constantly driven by the awareness that I had
to go further in my thinking.

Freud stated that the psychosis is a dream, and the dream a

psychosis, differing only in its early-morning reversibility. And of course we know that dream and psychosis are a regression. Psychosis, it is well known, is a manifestation of a return to the infantile period, and Bertram Lewin has recently given important evidence that the dream has an oral content. That means, therefore, that the psychosis has an oral content. The patient is telling us this again and again with every way he has of expressing the thought, "I am being poisoned." If this oral-regression concept is true, and we are well aware of the latent validity of all productions based on unconscious memories, then who is responsible for what the patient is feeling or, more correctly, reliving? Who is doing this poisoning? It must be the mother. One could argue that it is the father, but at this early neonatal period, the father is nonexistent in the eyes of the infant unless he is performing the rôle of the mother, and in that sense he is the mother. It might be argued that the infant has an innate wish to poison himself, a concept not discordant with the opinion of Melanie Klein, but although I have a deep respect for her investigations of the oral period, her concept of the infant directing hostility against himself, I cannot accept. To revert to our original premise: Very shortly after birth, the baby begins to distinguish between himself and the breast (bottle or other nourishing object). Quickly thereafter the realization comes to him that the breast is a part not of his mouth but of the mother. The woman (breast) with a healthy maternal instinct will unselfishly provide the infant with all the requisites of a comfortable and satisfying existence. There cannot be any poisoning from this breast, nor can the infant want to poison himself. Poisoning comes from the perverse mother who is not gifted with the divine attunement that makes her understand what her baby is crying for and allows her to return it to a world of omnipotent contentment.

Schizophrenia is a disease which has its inception somewhere between birth and prior to the termination of the pre-verbal period and is caused by the mother's inability to love her child. When the child expresses this faulty relationship to us again, now as a victim of the paranoid phase, he may hear the voices say, "You are rotten, you are no good, I hate you. Jump out of the window and get killed." So he expresses how he understood his mother's unconscious in the light of her instinctual failure. This failure results in a weak foundation for all the child's later development. It is like the leaning Tower of Pisa, to make a comparison. The Tower was built on a shallow, uneven foundation, and, as any construction engineer will tell you, it was fated for instability. It leans but fortunately does not collapse because it remains stationary at the point where it equalizes the force of gravity.

A human being cannot remain stationary. A child has to grow. If it has a parent suffering from a perverted maternal instinct, the child from the start must build on a weakened psychosexual base. Thereafter, at each critical period in development, the child will be shaken. It may survive and go on uncertainly struggling until it reaches the next point of severe environmental assault, let's say the oedipal period. Here the child may have to defend itself with a clearly defined clinical neurosis. If this is not efficient, there may result what is called childhood schizophrenia somewhere between the ages of 3 and 12. But suppose the child successfully negotiates this period, as it generally does. There now lies ahead the dangerous coming-of-age of puberty with the reawakening of the oedipal conflict. Now there is the added impact of full genital development and the threat of castration becomes imminent. The strain on the psychologic apparatus in withstanding what comes now is so enormous that the first signs of a break with reality appear: the beginning of regression to infancy, to the oral period, and some manifest psychotic behavior. This occurs at the age of 13 or 14, but there may be such a slight amount of schizophrenia that the individual can continue the leaning structure upward toward maturity. Points of threatening collapse will now be graduation from college, the marital experience, and, for men as well as for women, the birth of a baby—all periods of life accompanied by great amounts of psychologic stress. The birth of a baby means the individual is identified with the mother; so (the unconscious says) if you're the mother, who did you have intercourse with—Father. Punishment of incest in the unconscious is biologic death, a fate worse than death, and who is so strong that he can keep his psychologic balance in the face of such terrors? Certainly not the incipient schizophrenic. A child reared by a comparatively healthy mother may experience such unconscious terrors in dreams. With the awakening of the morning ego, healthy repressions come to the rescue, and the day's life ahead is a pleasurable experience. The child not so reared has no such resistances or psychologic fortitude and the unconscious material is constantly gnawing at the structure of the daytime existence. Coming after years of fear, after the wear and tear of fighting each successive onslaught, one can easily understand how the whole Tower of Pisa reaches a certain height, and then, no longer able to withstand the pull allegorically represented as the force of gravity, the whole psychologic structure crumbles back to what it started from, a shaky foundation.

The concept of the perversion of the maternal instinct fits every fact I have observed about the etiology of schizophrenia. It fits the behavior of the mothers of schizophrenics, it fits the material obtained from psychotic patients, and it fits the biologic fact that any instinct, in expressing itself, can become subject to perversion. Going through the gamut of instincts, I cannot think of one that is not subject to this law. I cannot think of one that cannot be bent to conform to the faulty aim-object relationship that we call perversion.

The gravity of this concept lies in the fact that, according to every indication, the impairment of healthy motherhood is heavily on the increase. The psychologist, sociologist, economist and anthropologist may each have his clue to this enigma. Our own psychoanalytic approach, based on clinical material from psychotic and neurotic patients helps us to understand why women wear men's clothes, try for commanding positions in business, and prefer not to care for their own children but hire nurses to play the role of make-shift mother. We also know that with the gratification of a perverted maternal drive, both the object and the one who exploits the object suffer. Our sympathies go out to both, but in this paper we are concerned with the infant.

What the infant suffers may have nothing to do with the conscious feelings or behavior of the mother. For example, a few days ago a woman called who stated, "I am the mother of Irene B. Shortly after becoming pregnant, she had a mental breakdown. At present she is in a sanitarium on Long Island under the care of Dr. K. She has received shock therapy and now the poor girl is in a terrible state. Dr. K told me that in his opinion, she is hopeless."

When I explained the extent to which my schedule was at present over-burdened and how sorry I was that I couldn't treat her daughter, she begged and pleaded in a most pathetic manner. She was relentless to the point of conducting a sit-down strike in my office. Her apparent sincerity was unquestionable, and it would seem that if giving her life could save her daughter, she would consent. Is it possible that such a woman failed to give her daughter the necessary love in infancy? I myself cannot consciously discern the non-loving qualities in this mother. Neither could anyone else. I don't doubt, however, that her daughter did, but how she did and what they were remains to be revealed through a searching analysis of this schizophrenic girl.*

Numerous psychologic studies, notably those of Levy, Ribble, Spitz, and Fries, have shown how difficult it is for parental attitudes of basic rejection and hostility to go unperceived by the child. No amount of conscious correction or unconscious overcompensation can conceal from the child the fundamental fact that it is unloved. Positive and negative thoughts and affects, no matter how minimal or how deeply repressed, can communicate themselves in ways which are far more direct and primary than anything we have heretofore imagined. This process, which is now being explored on many fronts, is presumably at its peak of effectiveness in the neonatal period when other means of communication between mother and child are relatively undeveloped

---

* Some years later, when the daughter was well enough to live at home again, the mother became overtly psychotic and tried to drown her daughter in the bathtub. This mother was treated with direct analysis by one of us, and the treatment was fully documented. She is one of the 27 cases recorded in the paper on prognosis in this volume. The point, of course, is that when the unconscious did manifest itself, there was murder in the air.

and where its biological utility would be highly important. The significance of this process in picking up and magnifying maternal affect distortions in relation to the infant is obvious. Where maternal rejection exists, it is inescapable and must necessarily be traumatogenic.

Freud said, "It is very remarkable that the Ucs [unconscious] of one human being can react upon that of another, without the Cs [consciousness] being implicated at all." Dr. Jule Eisenbud, in his studies of telepathic dreams, has adduced highly convincing evidence for the existence of such a means of communication.

Now the deeper explanation of the phenomenon of paranoid ideas in early schizophrenia suggests itself. The essence of paranoia is the feeling of being in primary emotional contact with people in the environment quite apart from ordinary means of communication. Beyond this behavior lie the vestiges of a period of life where this was indeed true, especially in relation to the primary libidinal object, the mother. What the paranoid is reliving in this symptomatologic form is the frustrating destructiveness of this early mother-child relationship which he now in his loneliness and isolation projects into the world at large. He is reaching out, groping, for a normal flow of love and sustenance from his environment, utilizing a mechanism biologically suitable for infancy, but he receives and perceives instead only hatred and death wishes directed toward himself.

This is a recapitulation of an earlier situation in which the child's needs disrupt the narcissism of a parent who, unable to love, responded with feelings or affects that amounted to, "Be still. Be quiet. Be dead."

An example of the importance of the early complete emotional nourishment of the child by the mother was unconsciously given by a mother who came to see me. Her daughter was a mute, rigid catatonic, and all the shock therapies and other procedures had failed to make a dent in the psychosis. After I agreed to take the case, the mother made the peculiar observation that the patient was simply run-down and that if she were allowed to give her daughter her own home-made chicken soup (the patient was hospitalized at the time), she would be all right. I took this patient out of the hospital and treated her. Every few days came a big jar of Mother's home-made chicken soup which was her method of showing her concern for her daughter by means of food. It was as if the mother understood unconsciously that this illness was in some way related to her earliest feeding experiences with her child. She apparently hoped that excessive food now would compensate for a flow of love that had not existed at the time when it was most needed. After resolving this patient's psychosis, I continued therapy with a more conventional analysis, and material obtained during the latter phase of treatment went a long way toward convincing me of the validity of my theoretic understanding. I found, for example, that the patient on one occasion had become momentarily rigid, felt unreal, and was for a brief period mute when the mother asked her to go to the grocery store and do her shopping for her. The free associations to this experience showed that the daughter became paralyzed with fear at the prospect of having to be a mother while being reminded that she herself had a mother who was no mother.

It is experiences like the above, happening again and again, that brought repetitively to my attention what I formulated in my opening sentence. Those who deny the perversion of the maternal instinct may still prefer an endocrine explanation, a vitamin explanation, a cosmic explanation, or will talk about minute neurophysiologic brain changes, or will again bring forward the ever-present constitutional factor. All except the constitutional factor have proved to be as meaningless as the masturbation theory which at the turn of the last century resulted in the bloody and shameless practice of castration as a therapy.

A final word about the constitutional factor. The rôle of this factor must be considered in any question of the etiology of human disease. In some diseases it plays a huge part. It was generally thought to play a large part in causing psychosis, but since nobody has been able to say exactly what its effect is, and since I have found it to play a minor rôle or no rôle at all in therapy, I find myself in disagreement with those who rely heavily on this explanation. As far as I can make out, the constitutional factor may give greater protection to one person than to another against a given injurious environmental experience, real or imagined. The same trauma may cause one individual to develop a neurosis and another to develop a psychosis, but by no means will the first individual be able to withstand unlimited amounts of assault without becoming psychotic. My knowledge as a general practitioner comes to my aid here. Where two persons are exposed to infection, one may not contract the disease. Unless a specific immunity exists, the chances are that the one who escapes does so by virtue of a constitutional factor. I have known such a patient who, on a second exposure to infection, was not so fortunate. Perhaps his constitutional factor deserted him, but most bacteriologists will conclude that the number and virulence of the disease-producing agents were just too much for him. To those who cite a constitutional immunization against psychosis, a word of caution may be offered about unlimited dependence on this safeguard.

In this paper I have stated my findings and conclusions. I hope with it to provoke the kind of healthy scientific curiosity that will eventually shed light where there is now so much darkness and bring hope where there is now so much fear.

PAPER 5.

The Survival Function of Schizophrenia

IN HIS PREFACE TO THE SCHREBER CASE, Freud said that "the analytic investigation of paranoia presents difficulties of a peculiar nature to physicians who, like myself, are not attached to public institutions. We cannot accept patients suffering from this complaint, or at all events, we cannot keep them for long, since we cannot offer treatment unless there is some prospect of therapeutic success." Most of Freud's energy and skill, therefore, was applied to the treatment and understanding of the neuroses.

Undoubtedly much of the confusion that arises in the discussions about whether psychoanalysis is applicable to the psychoses is due to the fact that the term schizophrenia has become a "catchall" classification which is used to describe everything from a borderline case with predominantly neurotic symptoms to a florid acute psychosis. The type of patient that I am talking about when I use the term "deteriorated schizophrenic" is one who would scarcely understand what I meant were I to ask him to follow the fundamental analytic rule of free association, to say nothing of his inability to focus his attention so that he could carry out this most intricate task.

Many years later, it was obvious that Freud had changed his concept of the applicability of psychoanalysis to the psychoses; he said, in *The Outline of Psychoanalysis,* "Nevertheless, it [the dream] is a psychosis, and we learn from it that even so deepgoing a modification of mental life as this can be undone and can give place to normal functioning. Is it too bold, then, to hope that it must also be possible to submit the *dreaded spontaneous illnesses* of the mind to our control and bring about their cure?"

Freud said that the dream is "the royal road to the unconscious." I think it is even more true to say that schizophrenia is the royal road to the unconscious. In the dream, one has the unconscious under scrutiny for a brief moment. In schizophrenia, the dream goes on and on and offers an unparalleled opportunity for study of the pathologic process without concern that it will suddenly be snatched from view. The unconscious material appears without interference from healthy resistances, exposing a variety of core conflicts which are only shabbily disguised. One of the insights which I have gained from continuous observation of these patients I wish to state in this paper.

I will use a patient's term, *imaginations,* to include delusions, hallucinations, and all the other instances of psychotic irrationality. Why do these *imaginations* take on the force of reality? Why is this system so unshakeable? No amount of logic, no pleading, no appeal to consider the welfare of others, not even the threat of burning at the stake, can shake such a construction. The delusion, like its anatomic counterpart, scar tissue, is much tougher and more impervious to destruction than the healthier parenchyma which it replaces. Surely there is serious purpose behind the schizophrenic construction. The unconscious may be accused of lack of judgment, but it cannot be accused of lack of function. What its total function is, I don't know, but one of its phases is becoming clear.

One patient who thinks his mother died 2,000 years ago is certain that this is so. Another who thinks he is Moses is equally certain. In a normal person, this false reality obtains in dreams, and here the dynamics are essentially the same as in schizophrenia. (It should be noted that imaginations with the force of reality may also be induced by drugs, toxins, and organic pathologic changes.)

The wish that something should be so is not sufficient in itself to produce the certainty described. Some wishes hardly make any impact on consciousness; others produce mild phenomena like daydreams. When a wish for something is so important that it involves a matter of life and death, then, and only then, does the unconscious part of the psychic apparatus spring into action and provide the necessary gratification with an *imagination*.

There is a story about a soldier, lost in the African desert, who almost died of thirst. He was found unconscious, with his mouth and throat full of sand. When he recovered he reported that he had suffered thirst for a number of days. Finally, wherever he looked he saw water and remembered falling down and scooping up handfuls of it, which were wet and cool to his touch and refreshing to taste. It seemed so real at the time that he found it hard to believe later that he had been drinking sand and not water. This recalls similar stories about starving, shipwrecked men who had fancied themselves enjoying sumptuous banquets, and about Alpine climbers, lost in blizzards, who had imagined themselves sitting around warm fireplaces in comfortable inns.

In these cases the wish for water, food or warmth was so urgent and the consequences of non-fulfillment so catastrophic that, at the point of physical collapse, the unconscious was able to provide imaginary food and water and warmth.

In these examples, I think we can find a condition common to all imaginative experiences which gain the force of reality: *A matter of life and death is involved.* If an *imagination* is experienced by a non-psychotic person as a psychologic response to a life-threatening deprivation, it seems logical to assume that the *imagination* of the psychotic is a psychologic response to something that *he conceives to be* a death-threatening deprivation.

Study of one of my patients who said, "I am Jesus Christ," revealed that his pre-psychotic life was involved with a story that he called "Hamlet Castle." Every thought in it concerned his enormous temptation to seduce his mother. While being consumed by the relentlessness of this intense wish, he was carrying on an unsatisfactory homosexual affair with his brother. His realistic behavior showed a constant preoccupation with incest and homosexuality. For him, it was the frying pan or the fire. Both threatened him with castration, i.e., biologic death. One can easily imagine how this conflict drained his psychologic energies and how much he wished to be normal and pure like other people. At the point of psychologic exhaustion and with biologic death imminent, he no longer merely wished he were pure, he became the purest of the pure. He identified himself with Christ, let his hair and beard grow, and became increasingly ascetic both in habit and appearance. He was safe at last.

Another patient, a woman in her early forties referred to herself as "The Holy Trinity." Although this patient was raised in a very religious community where all forms of sexuality were strictly forbidden to the "good girls," she exhibited herself to her brother and indulged in a good deal of homosexual play with a sister and a niece. When she married, she was able to tolerate sexual relations with her husband only if she could imagine that he was a negro. She gave birth to a daughter and was horrified to discover that she enjoyed handling the child's genitals. Her homosexual interest in her daughter provoked increasing anxiety, and for many years she lived in fear that she would die of heart trouble or of "some terrible disease." Doctors could find nothing wrong with her except an ulcer, which cleared up when she was put on a diet. She complained so much about her symptoms that her family finally took her to the Mayo Clinic where her complaints were diagnosed as psychosomatic. Several months later she became psychotic.

When the ego can no longer properly defend itself, the unconscious homosexuality threatens to emerge. In the unconscious, homosexuality is the equivalent of castration because both conditions preclude the continuance of the stream of life. When this homosexual attitude takes over, it constitutes the threat of imminent biologic death. At this point, in the case of the patient just mentioned, her *imaginations* gained the force of reality. She became the Holy Trinity, incorporating her masculinity, her femininity, and her child. She dealt with the instinctual drives that seemed to threaten her life, in a well-known paranoid manner, by saying that the tempting devil was responsible for all within herself that she felt to be evil. As the Holy Trinity, she was safe from the devil.

The wish, then, became schizophrenic reality because the consequences, from the patient's point of view, would have been deadly were it not satisfied. To further illustrate this mechanism of self-preservation and at the same time to show the type of crude and jumbled productions from which the basic motivation must be extracted by the therapist, I shall present some actual case material.

Case History

Joan, 25 year old mother of two children, was brought to my office in an acute catatonic state. She had on a dirty housedress and sneakers, and her long hair streamed untidily down her back. She was quiet only when she was preoccupied with some magical act, but, for the most part, she talked unceasingly in a rapid monotone, punctuated by gasps, tears, and inappropriate laughter.

During the first few visits, I listened carefully to her productions and told her often that I was there to protect her and would allow her to do anything she wanted to do. She crawled through the several doors in my office suite on her hands and knees. Each time she did so, she would squat down and press her abdomen, as if to give birth or to evacuate the bowels. She said specifically several times while doing this, "I have to give birth to me." Once when I asked her if she was in pain, she replied, "Christ, you don't have pain when you have a baby anymore." On one occasion she tried to crawl through a tiny opening in one of the windows; when she was unable to do this, she thrust her long hair through the opening. All her efforts seemed to be concentrated on a desperate effort to be reborn. Each time she went through this symptomatic act, it was interpreted to her as, *"You are trying to be born again. You would like to be a boy this time and maybe* then *your mother would love you."**

On the fifth day of therapy, I insisted for the first time that

---

* The schizophrenic wish to be reborn is nothing new. Girls often try to be reborn into boys. One of my patients said, "Somebody sewed up my hole. I think the doctor did it when I had my baby and my pee comes out through a tube attached to my belly button." This phenomenon is by no means limited to women patients. Men seek to become reborn as women, and, although I have had no such specific evidence as this in a male patient, I always find a homosexual fixation with the father figure as the object and the father's penis as the breast.

Joan stay in the treatment room with me. She stayed in the room, but when I asked her to sit down on the couch, she gave no indication that she had heard me. She wandered about the room gaily examining my books and furniture. Then, spying a cigarette on the table, she picked it up. When I said, *"Drop the cigarette,"* very firmly, she dropped it on the floor and made a dash for the door. I grabbed her, pulled her back in again, and forced her down on the couch. While I held her wrists, Joan squirmed, kicked, and wrestled violently. She kept up a continuous stream of productions which indicated she was fantasying enormous sexual experiences. The struggle lasted about half an hour, and I made no interpretations until she had quieted down from sheer exhaustion. Very often at the end of this type of struggle the patient seems closer to reality.

P: See saw, Marjorie Daw. [Sings.] Mother must get a new master.

D: *Have you got one now?*

P: Brother, you can say that again. Let him guess, he wants it. He threw it away, away, away, away. He threw it away, away, away. A minute, a moment. Girl, he broke my bones. I gave it the candle. You put it out. But it's out. Out. Out. Brief notes. Ooh, brief. Can this be brief? [Hums.]

D: *Lie still and don't move.* [Patient lies on stomach and bounces up and down, groaning in the pillow.] *Stop it, Joan!*

P: They don't know when the lights are out. I don't know when anything can possibly be worth such a bunch of crap.

D: *Stay right where you are.*

P: I don't know where I am. I am a little son out of the cunt. A.K. A.K. Break it again. In, in and out, in and out. That's what we don't see. We don't see it. Look at her arm. [Gasps.] Help, help, help, help, help. Pee. Oh, wait brother, I have to pee. If not, on the floor. That's all obvious. Well, look how obvious that object is. Object. Who has to scratch it? Her cunt. Pee on the floor. On the floor. No, there is a dark well that doesn't come back. It doesn't come back.

Nice little secretary, please. [Appeals to secretary in wheed-
ling tone.]

D: *She is only here to take notes.*

P: You must imagine. Oh—you don't know what you can
imagine in the dark, when you are so sick in the dark.

D: *Are you going to lie still now or does the fight go on?*

P: Yes, of course, if you will let me go. It wasn't worth it,
was it?

D: *No, it's better to lie down.*

P: Oh, rest. [Sighs.] Where is that son? Where is that son?

D: *Put your head on the pillow.*

P: My head on the pillow.

D: *Come on. No more fucking. Lie down. Put your head down
here. Pull your skirt down.*

The sexual experience that the patient has been enjoying is
probably only a feeling of bodily motion, perhaps being lifted up
by the mother or rocked in the cradle. At this level of regression,
I doubt whether there is any conscious genital feeling indicated
by her productions. I added *"No more fucking,"* which is an
interpretation on the genital level, rather than *"No more rocking,"*
in the hope of forcefully arousing the patient to more mature
considerations. This interpretation is probably incorrect for a
person so regressed, but by the use of this word, I hoped to
remind her of a genital experience she once had had, which during
the schizophrenic state is amnestic. All postphallic level experiences constitute a period of amnesia for the schizophrenic patient,
just as all prephallic experiences constitute an amnestic past for
the neurotic.

I told Joan several times that I was going to protect her but
that I also had to control her. I ordered her to lie still. She did
finally, and I asked her why she fought me when I loved her and
protected her. She put her left thumb in her mouth and sucked
it vigorously saying, "Ooh, that's good. That's wonderful. I
want it again and again." Then she removed this thumb and
sucked on her right thumb.

P: Out, out. He says to take the thumb out. Take it out.

D: *You have me mixed up with your mother. Did she tell you not to put your thumb in your mouth?* [Patient nods.] *Were you a thumb sucker as a baby?* [Patient nods.] *I don't mind if you suck your thumb.*

P: Thank goodness.

D: *That's all right. Don't bite it. You can keep it there as long as you want. It's all right. It's all right. Do you get pleasure from it?*

P: Yes.

D: *Is it very exciting?*

P: Yes. Yes. Hard. Hard. Hard. Hard. I love them. Christ, I love cigarettes. Why doesn't someone give me a taste, a taste. I want my thumb. I want my thumb. I can't have my thumb. It's nice to suck a thumb. A baby can certainly suck a thumb with its mother.

D: *I am your mother now, and I will permit you to do whatever you want.*

P: (Sucks thumb vigorously, breathing deeply and regularly.)

When I said, *"Drop the cigarette,"* the patient made a dash for the door like one in a panic. The cigarette is easily equated with the breast. In refusing it to the patient, I appear to the patient like the depriving mother must have appeared to the infant. The patient, enraged, then precipitates an enormous struggle, after which she seems closer to reality. I cannot go into the whole matter of schizophrenic aggression here because it is not the purpose of the paper to dwell on management of the patient. I will venture the following guess as to why it was necessary to win in this type of struggle with a patient.

The therapist, at this stage, is the forbidding parent. The patient hates the forbidding parent and wishes him dead. If the patient succeeds in this magical disposing of the forbidding parent, he himself is lost. Picture an infant at the breast level; imagine it alone in the midst of a forest in deepest Africa. As far as the neonatal infant knows, this might well be so because there is no one other than himself and his breast-mother as yet in his object world. If the parent is destroyed, what will happen to the infant? I credit the infant's unconscious with being aware that if the parent is destroyed it will then die. Perhaps this is based on the talion principle, perhaps not. At any rate, it has been my experience that the therapist must win or the patient will lose.

"See-saw, Marjorie Daw," is an experience of swaying to and fro, familiar to every child. At this patient's level of regression, it refers to infantile masturbation rather than to mature sexual intercourse even if she talks about mother getting a master. The word "master" carries with it the idea of one who is on top. The age of the "See-saw, Marjorie Daw" contains a whole world of discovery which includes the experience of early masturbation and the search for a more specific anatomic knowledge of the genitals.

"Oh, throw it away, away, away," could be a castration wish. "I gave it the candle," is a description of a well-known masturbatory experience. The birth concept of the Marjorie Daw child results in what the patient soon talks about: i.e., "A bunch of crap," which is herself being born. And then she states, "I don't know where I am. I am a little son out of the cunt." "I am a little son . . ." clearly indicates that *her wish has gained the force of reality,* and she now thinks of herself as a boy.

In connection with Joan's birth fantasies, it is well to pay heed to the teaching of psychoanalytic theory. From the experience of our analytic predecessors we learn that when a woman is giving birth, she unconsciously gains the equivalent of the longed for and hitherto absent penis.

Following the treatment up to this point, either because of the interpretations, the actual physical control of the patient's aggression, or because of other reasons unknown to me, her behavior changed. She was compliant and sat quietly on the couch. Her psychotic chatter no longer came in a steady stream, and she was able to converse with the doctor on a realistic level for a few minutes at a time. She allowed herself to be dressed more appropriately by the nurse.

Her psychotic productions became less irrelevant and now related mainly to her lack of a penis and her confusion regarding her sex. She still spent a great deal of time acting out birth fantasies. I interpreted her symbolic remarks and acts and constantly affirmed her femininity by calling attention to all her attractive feminine qualities, even insisting that her female genitals were far more useful and desirable than a male's. On the twelfth day of treatment, she giggled and said, "Gee, I think I am a lady, sir. That feels swell. Did we cut them deep in the groove?" I replied, *"Deep in the groove is your vagina. You have discovered that you are a woman."*

The next day, when she was all dressed up, Joan asked me if I didn't think she looked nice. Since she was calling my attention to her feminine attractions, I felt it was important to make a direct analytic response which would emphasize the desirability of being a woman rather than a man. *"Imagine how sad it would be if you didn't have your beautiful vagina. Your vagina has great value. It produced your two children. That's something wonderful that could happen only inside of your wonderful body. How I wish I could make a baby inside of my body."*

I could tell that Joan was impressed with my evaluation of her femininity, because from that moment on she ceased to give me the impression of clumsiness and heaviness. Her behavior became rather coy. She began to cross her legs and made obvious gestures of smoothing her clothes over her breasts and her hips to call my attention to these feminine virtues. There seemed to be no doubt that it did something to her pride in herself to know that I considered her an attractive woman.

Fifteen days after the start of treatment, Joan was well behaved and quiet. Her mind was still cloudy, however. She looked out of the window and wondered how it was that the city had been rebuilt so quickly. She remembered a short time back seeing it leveled to the ground. I told her that the city had not changed; she had changed. Then she spoke about her illness. She was under the impression that her eyes had been injured. She said at first, "Perhaps a change of glasses would straighten things out." (In the beginning of her illness she had seen strange things. She thought it was because of some visual defect, but I explained to her that whatever defect existed was to be found in her mind's eye. When she relinquished the psychosis and attained some judgment about reality, she resorted to a physical explanation of her illness and related it to an ocular abnormality. Many schizophrenics show this preoccupation with their eyes. Leaving aside for a moment what we know of the eyes in relation to castration, I would prefer to emphasize that a physical explanation provokes less anxiety than the psychologic one and it is through this hypochondriacal trick, even in early schizophrenia, that dangerous conflict material is kept in repression.)

Joan went on during this session to talk about her husband and described an encounter with him when she had refused intercourse. They had had a violent physical struggle, and she had won. I replied, *"You can be certain that between you and me, you will not win. I will win."* The patient answered, "I know that. We had our fight physically and mentally. You remind me of my step-grandfather." I answered (remembering the character of this man from the anamnesis), *"I guess he broke your spirit by overcoming you and dominating you when you were a child. The difference between him and me is that I dominate you to protect you from harm because I love you."*

The patient told me then that she didn't like me at all at first but that she became convinced I was on her side because I gave up my lunch hours for her and because I called her up on the telephone and seemed really concerned. Joan continued, "This whole illness is one of losing time. I went back as far as I could, even to my earliest infancy."

So much for the psychotic part of her illness. From here on, there was little of it left to deal with; it was obvious that she was awake.

Later, when Joan was being treated by a more orthodox form of psychoanalysis, the pattern of her early life gradually became clearer. Let me sketch Joan's case history very briefly.

She had struggled all her life to conform to the impossible

standards of a non-loving mother. Her mother demanded that she be pure, perfect in mind and body, and without sexual instincts. Joan must have sensed her mother's hatred* but, not understanding the hypocrisy of her mother's attitude, thought that if she could be all things that her mother wished her to be, she would be able to obtain her mother's love.

Her mother, she thought, loved her brother, who was three years her junior, and she observed that he was not forced to conform to the same rigid standards of behavior expected of her. The only difference she could see between her brother and herself was that he had a penis and she did not.

Joan's mother was unusually severe in regard to toilet training and infantile masturbation. Her mother had told her, when she was a child, of her father's disappointment that she was not a boy. In later years he displayed a disgust for her femininity that was almost pathologic. As long as she could remember, her father would make her stand in the light before she left the house, to make sure that her undergarments and her dress concealed the space between her thighs. This experience, which was very embarrassing to her and very difficult for her to relate to me, undoubtedly reinforced her feeling of sexual inferiority.

In a paper on technique, Freud states that the hardest thing to resolve in a woman's development is her penis envy; the hardest thing to resolve in a man's development, his homosexuality. Since experience shows that it is so difficult for women to resolve their penis envy under ordinary circumstances, it is no wonder that Joan was unable to resolve hers with the added burden of constant parental assault.

While at college in her late 'teens, Joan broke away from her family completely and a short time later, went to live with the man who was later to become her husband. Joan enjoyed the masculine atmosphere of the university and prided herself on being considered "one of the boys" among her lover's bachelor friends. She was unaware that her being one of this bachelor

* Her mother's hatred was unconscious and the real reason for it, I believe, could be discovered only by analyzing the mother. The same is true of the father.

group was related to her strong homosexual drives. This behavior no longer stood up in the face of her increasing involvement with this man. Unwisely, she got him to marry her and later moved with him to another part of the country where she soon found herself in competition with the women in their new circle of friends. This she was also unprepared to deal with for the same reason that she was unprepared to be married at all. Her husband pursued other women openly, but she refused to believe that he was unfaithful until she had actually witnessed an amorous meeting between her husband and another woman. This incident precipitated her psychosis.

Joan's psychotic *imaginations* represent a heroic attempt to live, just as did the *imaginations* of the dying soldier in the desert. Joan thought her mother could love her only if she were a boy, and because of Joan's life-and-death need to be loved by Mother, she sought to become a boy through symbolic rebirth. At Joan's infantile schizophrenic level, this meant, "Now Mother will feed me and I won't die." If this need to obtain Mother's love had not been so urgent, Joan would have experienced it simply as the thought, "I wish I had been born a boy, then Mother would love me more." Only when the need is a matter of life and death is sufficient energy generated to make the *imagination* real.

In looking back over this case and others like it, we see that the ego is playing a little game of make believe. The function of the *imaginations* is to provide the patient with those things that are necessary to the continuance of life. All that I have been reporting here will make no sense if you think of the schizophrenic as an adult, because the adult is unconcerned about getting food from mother. He can go to the icebox and get his own food, and he knows that. Considering the adult further, even if he commits incest with his mother, he knows that no one will castrate him. Only if you believe that the schizophrenic is again an infant will you be able to understand the life and death meaning of the deprivations he magically replaces, whether they be the breast, the stool, the genital, or anything else. The real parents failed to provide what it takes to insure proper development. If they had, it is my belief that the primary love objects could have been relinquished to the depths of the unconscious from whence they would not again have appeared in consciousness.

I will not attempt to bring out why the parents were unable to carry out their role satisfactorily, although I know that the answer to this question has far-reaching consequences. It makes clear, however, what the role of the therapist must be. Utilizing the transference and counter-transference, you become the patient's parent and the patient becomes your child. The patient is re-living the infantile period, and you are afforded the opportunity of bringing him up all over again. In the productions, you can discern what the patient wants. With words, deeds, and instinctual feelings you can replace the deficiencies that were experienced in the first place. My recovered patients tell me that I do this. I wish I could say exactly how and perhaps I will be able to in time.

Conclusion

In conclusion I wish to state that what I have emphasized in this paper is one facet of a complex process. The case material given may be interpreted in additional related ways. I have limited the emphasis to this one facet in order to make the single meaning or insight as clear as I could.

In the actual handling of a case, you deal with an interpretation pertinent to the moment, but direct analysis considers it essential to keep within therapeutic reach as much of the totality of the psychotic dream as one can possibly understand.

The Prognostic Outlook with Direct Analysis

THIS PAPER undertakes to describe what we know so far about the circumstances under which direct analysis works best. It also undertakes to point out that certain physical procedures usually interfere with, and sometimes make impossible, the use of this technique.

After six years of work and the treatment of approximately 100 patients, my colleagues and I became increasingly aware of certain ones who responded in a matter of a few months or less. These numbered 27 cases, or roughly a quarter of the total. It now became important to us to ask why results had been so markedly better with these patients. If all of them had been openly psychotic only for a brief period of time, the explanation would be simple. It would then be enough to say that the sooner you get to the treatment of the case, the easier it is to effect recovery. This does not seem to be true. One of the patients in this series had been ill for many years and recovered in a matter of weeks. What was significant with him, as with almost all the others, is that there had been no shock treatment. However, in contrast with the other cases, he had been institutionalized in state hospitals for the larger part of the 16 years of the florid illness. Other patients were institutionalized either briefly or not at all, or had been in private hospitals where it was well known that the entire personnel was geared to kind treatment of the inmates, if nothing else.

My experience with two particular patients, two 16 year old girls presenting the same initial degree of psychosis, may be suggestive. One of them, whose case I shall present in detail in this paper, did not have institutionalization or shock therapy and recovered from the psychosis in four weeks time. The other one received more than 400 shock treatments, mainly ECT but including also considerable amounts of insulin shock therapy, and has been treated by me with the same intensity for a period of close to two years, but the only visible improvement is in more accurate recognition of the people in her environment, return to the pre-psychotic status of being toilet trained, an interest in her clothing, and fairly decent table manners. Except for these manifestations of her improvement, the psychosis is almost as firmly entrenched as ever. This is not an isolated experience, but fortunately not many patients have come to me who have received 400 or more shock treatments. Generally the routine nowadays is 60 insulin coma treatments, preceded by or followed by 20 ECT, and some number of insulin shock combined with electro shock therapy. If this does not work, they double it and then keep the patient in status quo by maintenance doses of shock therapy, usually one a week.

Many patients come to me who have a history of having received more than 100 shock treatments; with these, it seems to me that the amount of shock treatment they have been called upon to withstand is directly related to the length and difficulty of treatment by direct analysis.

A number of attempts were made to treat patients psychologically who had received psychosurgery and to date I find these patients absolutely hopeless. I've thought here, if they cut these patients' heads off altogether, then surely the psychosis would be cured.

Every now and again, a patient is brought to us in a severely regressed state after almost completing the usual series of 60 insulin comas. Such a patient is so obviously getting worse that some member of the family becomes panicky and causes such therapy to be stopped. Sometimes the treatment of these patients is continued in psychologically oriented institutions where shock therapy has been abandoned. Some are cared for at home and occasionally they come directly to me. A few such patients defied our expectations of prolonged and difficult direct analysis and responded with the resolution of the psychosis within a few months. Why these patients did as well as the majority of cases whom I look upon as representing the best conditions for direct analysis, I do not know. (See Paper 3.) The important point for prognosis that arises from the facts so far given is that all patients who have not been shocked or have not been subjected to the cruelties of bad institutions respond rapidly to direct analysis. There has been no exception to this rule.

We have been taught to look upon the diagnostic categories as having an important prognostic significance. This is not so. The conventional categories of catatonia, hebephrenia, and paranoia tell us nothing which will help us to estimate the speed or even the possibility of recovery. What seems to us to be the key clue is the level of regression existing at the time the patient is brought to us. We have chosen the term regression rather than deterioration because deterioration has an organic connotation which has never been demonstrated and is misleading. In the term regression, reversibility is implicit whereas deterioration indicates a one-way negative process. I am willing to concede, however, that man-made deterioration which is irreversible results from shock treatment and lobotomy, but precisely what the influence is on the psychologic manifestations, I am not prepared to say.

In studying the cases of the 27 patients who represented the optimum conditions for the use of direct analysis, the outstanding impression we had of them was their capacity for verbalization, however bizarre. These verbalizations were loaded with paranoid ideas, and none of us had any particular difficulty in making the necessary interpretations. Most of these cases had only recently changed from a lifetime of severe neurotic or manic depressive behavior to the defense of psychosis, but some of them had maintained their level of superficial regression for decades. Generally speaking, the psychotic patient if benevolently dealt with, no matter how long he has been ill, will retain the capacity for intelligible verbal exposure of the unconscious and will not be driven to deeper levels of regression. Verbalizations are interesting from this point of view. The psychotic is reliving an infantile period of his life. We know about babies that some of them begin to talk at 9 months of age and others not until 2 or 3 years. It is to be expected that the 9 months old baby, although verbalizing, may be immature in the matter of toilet training, eating, walking, and dressing. It is more than likely that the 3 year old, although just beginning to talk, will have mastered these same training problems. At any rate it is to be assumed that he will have accomplished these tasks of maturity with a greater degree of efficiency than the 9 month old talker. This difference in the time of the infant's talking may account for the confusing fact that we frequently find psychotic patients who have retained the capacity to verbalize well but who are considerably regressed in other areas where you would expect mature behavior. By and large, it remains a fact that direct analysis generally does best with patients who have the capacity for easy verbalization of the unconscious.

Among the 27 cases mentioned above, where a good level of verbalization was observed, there were some departures from optimum conditions. Some cases spoke freely but not too coherently. Two had received some shock treatment. Of these two, one had been given five insulin injections, without coma, and the other, 11 shock treatments in a few weeks time. In neither case could we say that this amount of shock treatment had done any significant damage, nor could we say that the others in the series had suffered significantly from incarceration. In all cases, direct analysis was begun promptly and was based on an understanding of the problem as revealed by the psychosis.

Reference to the table of 37 cases in Paper 3 will show that, while some of these patients recovered rapidly, as discussed above, they did not fulfill our concept of the optimum conditions which led unfailingly to the resolution of the psychosis. Only those cases that did fulfill our basic requirements have been included in the 27 cases discussed in this paper.

In every one of these cases the resolution of the psychotic phase, as stated before, was accomplished in a matter of weeks, at the most a few months. After this relatively brief period, direct analytic therapy was no longer necessary. The patients then had regular appointments, could have their sessions on the couch, and could follow the primary analytic rule as well as any other patients do who have never been psychotic. Not a single one in this group defied psychologic therapy by failure to respond to direct analysis and not one went on to chronic malignant illness.

Three of these cases were treated by two colleagues and the recoveries of these patients have been equally gratifying. These three cases I include in this report because they indicate that the success of direct analysis does not depend upon any personal magic, but rather that this is a method which may be transmitted by training.

Case History

The most recent case which I dealt with personally, I propose to describe in some detail. Like the others in the series, it approximated the optimum conditions outlined, although the patient's regression had proceeded beyond the stage at which verbal productions were relatively coherent. Like the others, this case illustrates the kind of recovery that we claim can be secured if these conditions are met. That is to say, the patient—first seen last October—emerged from the psychosis after four weeks of treatment and is now undergoing the analysis which should result in immunization. Finally, the case described exhibits again what I mean by direct analysis. My selection from the almost complete stenographic record of the case shows the direct analysis in process. All through the treatment of the case, a group of my colleagues were present; their presence seemed not to interfere with the progress of the recovery.

The case which I shall describe had been diagnosed as schizophrenic by a psychiatrist who advised hospitalization if the patient didn't "come out of it" in the next few days. She didn't come out of it, and a psychologist, who was a relative of the family and whom they consulted on that basis, advised immediate commitment to a state hospital as the only hope. He diagnosed schizophrenia and said it would take at least three years before improvement could be expected. He thought immediate treatment imperative. That afternoon, the family took her to the psychiatric division of one of the city hospitals. Staff doctors here advised that the patient be committed to a state hospital, there to be treated with 60 insulin comas. Before this recommendation was carried out, the family contacted me and I advised removal to a private hospital where there would be no shock treatment. When my instructions were followed, I consented to treat the patient.

I first saw the patient, whom I shall call Mary, on October 14, 1949. She was lying in bed in the disturbed ward of a private hospital, to which her brother had had her transferred. She was in restraint. Not even long experience with mental institutions could make me oblivious to the shocking incongruity of her childish face in this unhappy setting.

Mary's facial expression showed quite clearly her confusion and her disconnection from what was going on around her. She seemed unaware of the other patients, doctors, and nurses. I inquired why she was in restraint and was told she had been eating her stool and chewing on her urine-soaked sheets. With the consent of the charge nurse, we removed her from restraint. I observed her for a few moments and noted that she was giggling, muttering, crying, and occasionally talking in a bizarre manner. She went through these various reactions with amazing rapidity. In some ways, her state reminded me of catatonic excitement, except that the unholy terror was absent.

That is what I saw. My preparation for the case had consisted of a study of Mary's history by means of interviews with members of her family. The history revealed an abundance of neurotic childhood patterns—it was a quite typical pre-schizophrenic history, from which I offer some highlights:

At about the age of 2, Mary developed what her mother described as peculiar fits of choking, during which she struggled for breath and turned blue. These attacks of choking, for which no physical cause could be discovered, occurred only when she ate. During the last and most violent attack, the mother suddenly remembered the doctor's advice—to insert her finger into the child's rectum. This terminated the attack, and it never recurred.

From that day on, however, the child developed severe and persistent allergies which finally brought her to an allergy clinic. Tests showed that she was allergic to "almost everything."

At the age of 5, Mary began to annoy her brother by persistent pestering and teasing. He discovered a remedy for this. When he pushed her into the bathroom, she would cry hysterically for a few minutes and then would come out and leave him alone.

When Mary was 7, she began a peculiar ritual. She could not go to sleep until she herself had closed all the drawers and doors in her room. This developed into a compulsion to see that all the windows and doors in the apartment were locked and that all the doors and drawers in closets and cabinets were shut tightly. When asked why she did this, she said, "I'm afraid a mouse will come out."

When Mary was about 8, her behavior began to be disturbing in school and her school work deteriorated. She talked incessantly and rapidly; she fidgeted; she had poor coordination and balance and was generally considered very clumsy. The family, the neighbors, and the people at school began to refer to her as a "nervous" child.

At the age of 9, Mary stopped her nightly ritual but developed what was described to us as a behavior disorder. She wouldn't go to bed when the rest of the family retired, and for years there were violent scenes between mother and daughter every night at bedtime. The screaming and yelling were so violent as to disturb the neighbors. This embarrassed the mother. When it got too bad, the father would go out for a walk. One night, during such a scene, the mother, in a fit of fury, seized a broom and threatened to strike the child with it. Mary was so astonished at this show of violence that she accepted the necessity of going to bed. Thereafter her protests against going to bed were mild.

In her tenth year, Mary began to complain that people picked on her. Her constant accusations were accompanied by considerable affect and finally by hysterical outbursts of crying in school. Apparently this behavior was so unprovoked as to cause the teacher to announce in class one day that there was something wrong with Mary and that she should be taken to a psychiatrist.

When Mary's conduct came to the attention of the principal of the school, he wisely suggested that all she needed was more love and affection, particularly from her mother. Things were not set right by this advice, however, and because of her behavior, Mary's playmates called her by such nicknames as "Idiot," "Crazy," and "Dopey."

At the age of 12, Mary began to menstruate. Precisely at this point, she began to show evidence of regressive changes. Outstanding among these were that her mother had to dress her, and with each period her mother had to put on her sanitary napkin. At the age of 16, when I first saw Mary, her mother still dressed her every day and took care of her menstrual hygiene.

At about 13, Mary began to complain that the girls in her group were making up and spreading vicious lies about her. Her teacher suggested to the mother that it would be better for Mary to go to a different school.

In June, 1949, in Mary's sixteenth year, her brother married. At the wedding Mary became tremendously excited and had an extraordinarily good time. A short time later, when her family was shopping for a television set, she became almost hysterical over the prospect of owning one and could talk about nothing else night and day. In August, her parents took her to the country for a vacation. In this region there was an Indian cemetery, and Mary ran from monument to monument in great excitement, asking, "How are they? Where are they?" She was very much interested in Indians and talked about them a great deal.

Several weeks after Mary returned to school in September, she came home crying so convulsively that her mother became frightened. Mary reported that one of the children in her class had given her a piece of candy which she spit out because it had a peculiar taste. She said the candy was "poisoned." Her story was confused and it could not be determined whether or not her friends had played some kind of trick on her.

This event seemed to precipitate the patient into a considerable break with reality. That evening her sister noticed that Mary spoke in half-sentences and began to ask her mother over and over again for definitions of "common sense" and "worry." She asked whether it was possible to get leprosy and cancer from worrying. The following day, Mary announced that she had made a great invention that had to do with pulling up the shades in the classroom so that it was unnecessary to use electricity. She said that men were being sent to the school to fix all the shades. The mother asked her what she was talking about and the patient explained, "I'm an inventor. I have invented a lot of things. I'm going to invent color television, too."

This was the point at which the mother realized that the girl was insane and took her to a psychiatrist. This is a convenient point at which to summarize:

Prior to the onset of the psychosis, Mary had gone through a series of well-differentiated neurotic states. The first and earliest of these could be called a psychosomatic disorder, i.e., the globus hystericus and the allergic phenomena. These defenses were insufficient to arrest the progress of the illness. She developed a deeper modification, i.e., the obsessive-compulsive ritualistic behavior, a more severe manifestation of mental illness. Again this proved unavailing, and the ego sought a level of defense closely approximating overt psychosis: suspiciousness and paranoid trends. With the collapse of this level of defense, we find the outbreak of overt psychosis.

With the patient before me in a state of enormous excitement, and with this history in mind, I had to decide where to begin. My reasoning was as follows:

If left to her own devices, she would put anything in her mouth. She couldn't stand the loss of anything—stool, urine, her brother to his new wife, being deprived of a penis, losing her mother to her father, losing her father to her mother—or anything else.

Although the foregoing deprivations are unquestionably of prime significance, in the schizophrenic one must go deeper. The castration that counts is the loss of the breast. Not only as a breast, but as a symbol of all the homeostatic functions of mother, conscious and unconscious, that mean life to the neonatal baby. I reviewed the history: for years she had shown a tendency to regress. With the onset of menstruation, she behaved like a baby again. She couldn't dress herself or put on her sanitary napkin. Her mother had to do this for her.

The candy was poison. Perhaps she was reliving her earliest experience at the breast, when her mother's unconscious behavior was poison in another sense. Eating the stool and urine means that she was at that infantile level where babies can stand no bodily loss. She tries to replace it through her mouth. Just prior to this in her infantile life, wasn't the breast a part of her body, and wasn't the infant one with the mother's breast? Didn't she feel the loss of the breast as a castration with the most enormous consequences? Wasn't she struggling as anybody would to protect herself from such a significant loss? Why shouldn't she struggle? The need to get something into her mouth was a matter of life and death. Right or wrong, my initial interpretation was that what she wanted was the assurance of a steady flow of milk.

I decided not to interpret the castration except on the earliest oral level. There was a reason why through the years she was constantly struggling to regress. It wasn't just to have her mother dress her. She was out to recapture her earliest infantile relationship to her mother. It would give her a chance to try again. Perhaps this time she would get what she hadn't gotten when she was truly an infant. She would have another opportunity to overcome dissatisfaction that she originally felt at the breast and that had left an impression on her whole development—a void.

I took Mary's head in my hands, forced her gaze on mine and said: *"Don't worry, I won't let you starve."*

She replied, "Somebody did anyway. Some cat. Well, I don't care. I stuck to my religion."

I said, *"You mean you stuck to your mother."*

Mary answered, "I know that, too, but still I stuck to her and still I had my religion. Don't you know you got to breathe first? I just told you, I'm cleaner than everybody else."

She had heard me say that she wouldn't starve. When she said, "Some cat," I thought it probably referred to her mother. When she said, "I stuck to her," I was sure I was on the right track. Mary's reference to "cleaner" and "religion" gave me my cue to proceed. These are words which indicate a reaction formation against all kinds of dirt and all kinds of evil. If she's clean and she doesn't soil and wet, perhaps then mother would love her and she would be assured a steady flow of good milk. If she doesn't touch her genitals, she will be clean and her mother will love her and she will be assured a steady flow of good milk. If she doesn't have evil thoughts toward her brother and her father (that is, if she obeys her religion and doesn't permit herself such evil), her mother will love her and she will be assured a steady flow of milk.

One more point. She leads me from the oral to the anal level. That's plain. What can I say about clean and dirty and religion? We know from the history that she pestered her brother at the oedipal period—more than ordinary pestering. This is demonstrated when at her brother's wedding she behaves in a hypomanic fashion. Does it require much of a stretch of the imagination to read the incestuous thoughts between the lines? I was prepared to interpret further and by so doing show her my understanding of her problem. I told her, *"It isn't dirty to want to have intercourse with your brother. It's not dirty to want your father to make you a baby. I won't punish you for these things. Perhaps your mother won't love you, but I will."*

The case continued like a fugue; the same theme repeated itself again and again with only minor variations. On October 17, the fourth day of direct analysis, came the first sign of what Dr. Jan Frank so aptly calls, "the distancing of the patient from the psychosis." She was crying and suddenly stated, "My grandpa told me not to be frightened." She embraced me and asked me what my name was. I told her, and she said, "Oh! Somebody said something."

Heretofore Mary had talked as if in a dream. This remark consisted not only of the dream state, but also of a direct reference to somebody in the real world who says something. She had distinguished my voice from the dream voices. Greatly encouraged, I wanted her to understand me as distinguished from the voices. I implored, *"Listen, sweetheart! Mary! What are the voices saying to you now?"*

She replied, "The concert, it goes all the way down, the concert. It's two figures in one or something. I don't know what they mean by that."

D: *Listen to the voices now and tell me what they say.*

M: Go to your dentist. Go to the doctor and never let anyone play a prank on you.

D: *But the girls played pranks on you in school and at the party.*

M: Yeah.

(This last reference is to reality. It is necessary to strain mightily to try to bring the patient to reality when the slightest opportunity presents itself. I refer to her schoolmates playing pranks on her because we learned from her family that they had actually done so.) The conversation continued:

D: *They were mean to you. There are mean people in the world, just like your mother.*

Except for week-ends, when I did not have stenographic assistance, the verbatim record of this case is quite complete. I wish I had time to detail all the fine points of therapy in it. Every day the patient moved closer to the orbit of reality. On October 21, the eighth day, Mary knew that she was sick, but she thought she had polio and that I was a dentist.

M: So who got the polio, dentist? I got to suffer. She just waked me up. I can't help it.

D: *Stop talking crazy.*

M: It don't sound crazy yet.

D: *Yes, it does.* [Patient mumbles.] *You're still crazy.*

M: No.

D: *You don't even know who I am.*

M: A dentist.

D: *No, I'm not a dentist.*

M: I know you.

D: *What is your name, please?*

M: [Gives correct name.] She's a genius. I have polio. How do you cure that?

D: *You wish you did have polio. You would rather have polio than realize what your real trouble is.*

M: No, but I was sick. How do you get over this?

D: *I am a psychiatrist.*

M: Are you sure you're Jewish—the way you talk?

D: *I said that I was a psychiatrist.*

M: And I said, God himself told it to me.

D: *What did your father tell you?*

M: Nothing. I was born a Jew.

D: *Who cares?*

M: So you're probably the crazy one.

D: *No, you're the crazy one.*

M: I know. How do you go about curing it?

D: *Well, I'm a psychiatrist and I know how to cure.*

M: How do you do it?

D: *By talking.*

M: Go ahead and talk.

D: *I'm trying to find out what made you crazy.* [Patient giggles.]
   I think your mother did it.

M: I was nervous all the time.

D: *I know. I don't think your mother cared for you.*

M: How do you know?

D: *I know your mother.*

And so we continued. On the twenty-fourth of October, the
eleventh day of treatment, I asked her to tell me what had happened to her. She replied, "I was supposed to be a queen bee or
something. I don't know." Notice that the patient is being drawn
closer and closer to the realization of the true state of affairs,
and her imaginative thinking is rapidly diminishing.

On the twenty-fifth of October, Mary said, "I know I'm sick,
but still I don't know what it was."

D: *Well, I told you what it was yesterday, didn't I?*

M: Yes, if I was here yesterday.

D: *You were here yesterday. What was it?*

M: Oh, I don't know.

D: *What was the sickness that you had?*

M: Some kind of fear, I think. Somebody seems to think we have
   polio. I don't know.

D: *The fear you had, all right. There's no question about that, and you started to have a dream that you couldn't wake up from. I think you're still dreaming.*

M : No.

D : *When did you wake up? Do you know what the sickness was?*

M : Josephine K's [her mother] daughter. I don't understand it. I didn't have polio?

D : *That has nothing to do with it.*

M : I can't say. I don't know.

Up to November first, there was little change. I had gotten confirmation from the patient of a connection between her mother and her mental illness. On this date, when she was somewhat clearer and knew my name and the name of the hospital in which she was staying, I again persuaded her to explain her sickness to me. I asked her why she was sick. After some reflection, she said: "I think it was me."

D : *You think it's you? Well, if it's you, you can change it, can't you? If it's her, there's nothing you can do about it. I don't think it was you. Would you blame a baby if a mother doesn't love it?*

M : No.

D. *That's your answer, It's pretty tough to face that fact. When I asked you during the insanity what was the matter with you, you said, 'Josephine K's daughter,' as though you realized that it was your mother.*

M : She is.

D : *I know, but when I asked you what your sickness was, you said, your mother.*

M : I don't remember what happened every day.

D : *I know you don't, but I remember very well. It was during the insanity, while you were dreaming, that the truth came out. The truth that you didn't know about.*

M : Tell me. I don't understand the idea.

D : *In a few days I'll let you go home from the hospital and then you will come to my office. Then I'll explain it to you.*

M : I don't know. Because I'm a girl scout?

This last turning back to imaginations again is almost a therapeutic confirmation of the correctness of our assumptions. When I touch upon this significant injurious agent, her mother, she retreats and makes an irrelevant reference to being a girl scout. I was not concerned because I had confidence in the extent to which the therapy had already immunized her. If she had not found me an adequate parent, she would not have come this far. She was transferred to the open ward. She ate with the other patients, and the nurses reported that she was mostly in reality and was getting on well. It didn't go in a straight line toward success, but the major trend was in the right direction.

On November 4, 20 days after the beginning of the direct analysis, we had the following conversation:

D: *Do you hear voices?*

M: Yes.

D: *What do they say to you?*

M: I hear everything all right.

D: *I mean, when no one is around, do you hear voices in the air?*

M: No, I don't think so.

She acts as though my question were absurd, and ridicules the idea of voices, which means that she's disturbed by a feeling of shame—a very healthy ego function.

On November 6, as I continued my pressure toward reality, I called Mary's attention to the fact that in the three weeks that she was in the hospital her mother had not come to see her once. The patient fainted dead away. I should say, in all fairness, that the mother had been acting on my orders. Perhaps a harsh procedure but not as harsh as schizophrenia. My purpose was to focus the patient's attention on the pathogenic lack of love rather than to allow her to be confused by the mother's loving attitudes.

On the following day, November 7, we discussed this.

D: *What made you faint yesterday?*

M: I don't know. I just didn't feel good.

D: *What was it? What was in your mind the moment you started to get faint?*

M: I got dizzy. I don't know.

D: *Do you know where you are and what's been happening?*

M : Yes. [She mentions the name of the hospital.]

D : *What is this hospital for?*

M : For mental and nervous cases.

D : *Why are you here?*

M : To get better.

D : *What's the matter with you?*

M : Nothing. I don't know. I was just sick.

D : *What is the sickness? Don't hesitate to tell me.*

M : I don't know.

D : *What is your sickness?*

M : I was nervous. I was upset. I don't know.

D : *I don't like a liar.*

M : No, I don't lie. Why should I lie to you?

D : *Because you want to hide the fact that you were crazy.*

M : So? Well, I'd rather not tell it to anybody.

D : *Well, you can tell it to me. Don't lie to me again, Mary.*

M : My mother didn't come.

D : *She will come.*

M : Why didn't she come during the week?

D : *That's why you became crazy—on account of your mother.*

M : I don't know. I am very stupid.

D : *No, it's not your fault. It's her fault.*

M : She was probably very busy out there. We live in Brooklyn.

D : *I don't like this business of your trying to make believe. During the insanity you went on an imaginary journey.*

M : I went to a hospital.

D : *I don't mean really. I mean in the imagination. You felt you were all over the world.*

M : I was an Indian queen.

D : *If you were the queen, you were married to the king. That way, in your imagination, you could be married to your father. The father is always king.*

M : I love him. I just wanted—It was a sad day.

D : *The truth hurts.* [The unresolved oedipal longings appear to be felt more keenly by the schizophrenic than by the neurotic.]

On November 11, I spent more time than usual with the pa-

tient. It was my last visit with her. The productions were sensible.
She could answer any questions relevantly, and she was anxious
to go home.

D: *I'm going to allow you to go home.*

M: When?

D: *I think I'll have your mother come and get you sometime
today.*

M: I won't do anything foolish again.

D: *I guess you told me that to make sure that I would send you
home.*

M: It's up to you. I feel all right.

I explained to Mary that I was going to arrange for another
psychiatrist to take care of her, but I assured her that I would
be constantly available and always in touch with what went on.
When she kissed me good-bye, she had tears in her eyes, and
there was no question in my mind about how she felt. There
was no question about how I felt, either.

The duration of the treatment was exactly four weeks to the
day. No day's treatment lasted more than two hours, and on many
days considerably less time was spent with the patient. At the
end of the period, the patient was discharged from the hospital
and immediately began regular psychoanalytic sessions with a
psychiatrist who has had considerable experience with analysis
of children and adolescents. The last report from the psychiatrist,
dated January 27, is entirely satisfactory. The patient spends her
hour dealing with material such as her education, her relationships
with other members of the family, her social experiences (which
include dates), how to behave with boys, and optimistic thoughts
about some day being happily married and having a family of her
own.

Mary was examined in my office on February 13. One of my
colleagues who had witnessed most of the treatment sessions was
present. Before Mary came, she told her mother that I was very
cloudy in her mind and admitted that she was nervous about
seeing me again. I asked her many searching questions to determine the extent of her insight and judgment. She recalled the

period of her psychosis vividly, but referred to it as being "like in a dream." She said that she no longer felt that way, and I convinced myself that she was not saying this to prove to me that she was all right. She talked freely about how nervous she was with me and even expressed surprise that her hands were wringing wet from nervousness. She said that the most frightening thought she has now is that in some way she may get sick like that again. I reassured her on this score, confident that the analysis would be successful and that her fears would prove baseless. Mary has been living at home since her discharge from the hospital, and her family reports enthusiastically on her present adjustment.

Summary

During the past six years, we have been treating mainly cases of schizophrenia which had proved resistive to the usual forms of organic therapy. By constantly reviewing and discussing our findings we were struck by the fact that from the total number treated, 27 responded with marked rapidity. For the most part, these 27 cases differed from the others significantly in that: (1) They had had no shock therapy, except as mentioned above. (2) They had not been subjected to the usual manner of incarceration. (3) They were capable of conventional verbalization.

A most pertinent question raised by our present findings is this: What is "so-called deterioration," and to what extent is it a man-made consequence in schizophrenia, that is, the result of approved but really unwise and harmful therapeutic practices?

As in other fields of investigation, the areas of psychiatry we do not understand appear to exceed those we do. Yet we know a good deal. It is important to have learned that schizophrenic psychosis can be resolved through the psychologic approach of direct analysis. Once the resolution of the psychosis brings the patient back to his original neurotic state, a more orthodox type of psychoanalysis is applicable and should be followed until the individual is firmly secured against a recurrence.

Discussion of Treatment Techniques

When I started my work with schizophrenic patients, I was struck first of all by the therapeutic value of direct interpretation, probably because my first experience was with excited catatonic patients where the effectiveness of direct interpretation was dramatically highlighted. Because it was the most conscious part of the method and formed the bulk of the case records, it was the most easily isolated of all the complicated factors in therapy. Although I now know I was doing intuitively many other things that contributed to a successful outcome in my early cases, my original papers stressed direct interpretation and passed very lightly over the many other therapeutic devices that I have come to regard as perhaps equally important and without which interpretation loses much of its effect. Earlier in my work, when I discussed direct analysis, I was inclined to call everything I said to the patient a direct interpretation. I did not make a distinction between the kinds of interpretations I made, nor did I always make explicit the context in which the interpretation was given.

Reflecting over the beginning of my work with psychotics, I am surprised that any of my contributions continue to be valid. Every beginning in life is difficult, whether it be the earliest developmental phenomena of walking, eating with proper table manners, the first arithmetic lesson, or the more highly complex beginnings of one's life work in relation to one's fellow men. Therapeutic experience in direct analysis is so intense and the involvement with the patient so extreme that one is just about completely absorbed in it while it takes place. Trying to understand what has been done requires judgment about an emotional experience after the fact. My first papers went as far as I could, but their tentative findings brought them under critical fire from many psychiatrists to whom the whole idea of a psychologic approach was entirely foreign and irritating, and even from a number of experienced analysts who were sincerely interested in my work, but who did not find the same reactions to interpretations that I found. The reason why I had been having a different result was evidently the existence of factors which were only suggested by my papers or perhaps were not given at all.

In this paper, I should like to describe in detail some of the therapeutic techniques of direct analysis.

I should like, first of all, to call attention to the function of schizophrenia. So far as the patient is concerned, it is not simply something that happens to him; it is the way he must live in order to survive. The purpose behind schizophrenic behavior is to control in some magical way those aspects of the environment, external as well as internal, that are too oppressive for the patient to face as they really are. We must realize right from the start that the patient is schizophrenic because he desperately wishes to be and that he's not going to be kindly disposed to having his sickness interfered with. He wishes to be schizophrenic because there is something he cannot get from his environment that he can find in his imagination. However inadequate the imaginary substitute may be, it answers an essential need, and he clings to it tenaciously.

Although his illness may have a survival function, the schizophrenic patient is trapped in a relentless nightmare from which there is ordinarily no waking up unless something positive is done about it. We, as therapists, have to give the patient both a motive for, and a means of, returning to reality.

Before discussing specific techniques, I should like to state again what I call the overriding principle of direct analytic therapy: that the therapist must become to the patient the ever-giving, ever-protecting maternal figure. In order to give the patient conviction about your rôle as loving mother, it is absolutely necessary that you feel this way and that you communicate it unconsciously to the patient. One cannot pretend, but one can acquire this feeling unconsciously through identification with the patient. It is as if one said to the patient's unconscious: "I feel as you do, and I know what you want. I understand that you need certain things. Inasmuch as I am like you, I will attempt both to be you and to be your protector at one and the same time." You give the patient an opportunity to hallucinate on you, rather than on thin air, where there has been no object relationship with the world of reality. Only if the therapist is able to provide love and protection, only if he can convince the patient that he really understands his needs and is prepared to satisfy them, will the patient dare to wake up.

The purpose of direct interpretation is to make the patient feel understood. When you make an interpretation that is correct, the unconscious portion of the patient's ego, particularly in a florid schizophrenic psychosis, will know that you understand him. The feeling of being understood is of enormous therapeutic value, just as it is with a baby. When the baby cries, you have to know what to do about his cry. If the baby cries because the diaper pin is sticking him in the buttocks and you give the baby a bottle instead, you don't understand what the baby wants and you will not stop his crying. The schizophrenic is trying to hallucinate the diaper pin away, but he also cries for help, and you have to help him correctly.

When making a direct interpretation, the assumption is that the symbolic representation of the id has a meaning in the sense that manifest dream material has a meaning. We interpret it accordingly, drawing on our experience of what the psychotic dream means, in verbal productions or other manifest behavior, and we try to convey our understanding to the patient in any way that we can. For example, if a patient paints her eyes with lipstick, we understand that since lipstick is something you paint your mouth with, she is bringing her mouth in contact with her eyes. What we would like to do is try to make the patient understand, with whatever conscious ego remains, that to her unconscious her eyes represent breasts. Sometimes the patient will even help us to understand this because the eyes at different levels of psychosexual development can represent other things. They can represent testicles at the phallic level of development, for example. But the earliest knowledge is not of the phallus but of the breast, and the idea to get across is that the patient wants to nurse, wants to attach her mouth to those eyes (breasts). Bearing in mind Freud's understanding, the infant feels in the beginning that the breast is a part of its own ego, simply an extension of the mouth. The schizophrenic, always deeply regressed to the earliest oral level, understands and feels things with the affect that belongs to ideas of the neonatal period, the beginning of life's development. Sometimes the patient herself may furnish the answer. We might ask, *"Why did you paint your eyes with lipstick?"* And she answers, "That tall woman with the green skirt wearing an embroidered blouse." *"Who is that tall person?"* "Her name is Jenny." Since Jenny is the name of the patient's mother, she is telling you some thoughts about her mother. If our assumption is correct, it is as though the patient said, "I had a great deficiency at the oral level. I never had enough breast." Not that she wasn't well fed; she may have been overly well fed, if the mother was defending against her disinclination to feed the child, but what this baby felt about the attitude of the mother is something the baby would only perceive unconsciously. It is not necessarily true that the mother consciously can be distinguished from any mother with healthy maternal instincts. But, obviously, in this mother's unconscious existed certain feelings that the patient is now complaining about. "I didn't get enough of X, that I should have had at the time I was an infant, when my life depended on my mother's being this way or that way toward me."

I have often been asked, what is the basic difference between a direct interpretation and any other analytic interpretation? In a good analytic interpretation, you listen to the patient for about six months and then you say something to the patient which was obvious to you immediately. You could have made a direct interpretation at the very first interview, but with a neurotic patient it would have fallen on deaf ears. There is no neurotic patient who hasn't heard that he had an Oedipus complex and that he wanted to have relations with his mother. They are very interested, often agree with you, and say something such as, "I understand that, yes, doctor, that's so." But an interpretation of this type would make no real impression on them. They are only ready for it after the six months of work. The schizophrenic patient is ready at once. Everything that is ordinarily hidden from the conscious ego is apparent with him. In fact, I once saw a schizophrenic man in his thirties leap on his 76 year old mother, ignoring appealing young women who were present. In making a direct interpretation, the therapist can often penetrate through the thinly disguised symbolism and get to the heart of the matter, to the core conflict. With the neurotic patient, as Freud said, you have to "peel down the layers" until you get enough of the unconscious exposed so that the interpretation can be reacted to.

Frequent as the receptiveness of the schizophrenic is, it does not always exist. Even interpretations for which one has overwhelming evidence and which should be immediately apparent to the patient, do not always work. Much depends on whether the level of the interpretation you make is geared to the patient's level and whether the patient is emotionally prepared to accept it. It depends very much on whether you are dealing with a very anxious patient or with a paranoid patient who has a very well walled-off delusional system, with the rest of the personality almost free from any evidences of schizophrenic symptoms (i.e., fundamental symptoms in the Bleulerian sense). Such a patient is like an individual with a very well calcified and walled-off tubercular lesion. The patient is not suffering from fever or from many of the other things that would exist if the infection were not walled off. This type of patient would have to be handled in a very different way from the schizophrenic patient who is almost in a maniacal state of excitement. With the paranoid patient you have to confirm the delusional system and then try to find a way to undermine it in order to promote anxiety, whereas with the other type of patient the anxiety is very apparent.

Even when an interpretation seems to make no impression on a patient, you will notice, if you persist in confronting him with reality (unmasking his symptoms, delusions, etc.), that it becomes increasingly difficult for him to defend his psychosis, much less get satisfaction out of it. I can think of a parallel experience in connection with my own little girl. Several years ago up in the country, she was playing grocery store with other children in the neighborhood. She didn't come when she was called for dinner and I became annoyed. I told her to throw away the stones, the sand, and the make-believe money and come in. She objected, and I said, "Now don't be silly, that's sand not sugar, and those are stones, not bread, etc." I noticed that she didn't obey immediately and tried to keep on playing grocery store for a while, but it didn't work. The truth had disturbed the imagination and spoiled it. The game had lost its charm, and she couldn't enjoy it any more.

Other times direct interpretations bring about a shift in the symptoms. For example, an obsessive-compulsive male schizophrenic patient kept bending his arm at the elbow and I said, *"What does that mean?"* He replied, "If I do that, the hollows disappear from my arms." I answered, *"If you don't have a hollow, you're not a woman,"* and he stopped doing that and began moving his hand in front of his ear. I thought he didn't want to hear what I had to say, that he had a castration fear, but it didn't mean that at all. Having disturbed the imagination about one hollow, he immediately went to another one, his ear. I asked him what he was doing, and he said, "You're shooting germs at me, and they are jumping into my ear. I don't want that. I've got to block it." He had displaced the symptom almost immediately from the vagina in his arm (the idea of a hollow) to his ear and defended there against his wish to be a woman, the assumption being that he had to reassure himself that he was not castrated, that he was not a female, and that he had not lost anything precious. The patient shifts his symptoms like this again and again when you make an interpretation; he jumps nimbly from one area protecting his unconscious conflict to another. In certain cases you have to just run through the gamut till you exhaust the maneuvers of the unconscious ego.

The interpretations I have explained and illustrated thus far have been, strictly speaking, direct interpretations, where the therapist's relationship to the patient may be implied but is not made explicit in the interpretation itself. By and large, however, most of the interpretations I make are transference interpretations in which I interpret the patient's behavior in terms of my emotionally charged maternal or paternal relationship to him in the treatment situation. For example, as one of my patients, a young woman, improved, she revealed an enormous homosexual component. She went to Brooks Brothers and bought a man's suit, socks, shoes, and hat, and then bobbed her long hair almost to a crew-cut. She really is a beautiful girl, and I was horrified and hurt when I looked at her. I told her that I could never love her now unless she became a woman again. I wouldn't look at her. I wouldn't have anything to do with her. I told her I didn't want a son, I wanted a daughter. She meant everything to me as a daughter, and here she had double-crossed me and become a boy. The obvious interpretation would have been, "You are trying to become a boy." But had I said that, I would have remained outside of the psychosis; I would not have engendered that close feeling that is so important to make an interpretation really felt by a patient. The patient knew she wanted to become a boy. What she had to learn, not only in so many words but through my emotional reaction to her metamorphosis, was that I loved her as she was, as a girl.

In the case of the young man mentioned above, who was pushing germs out of his ear, I didn't say, "You don't wish to become pregnant." Nothing of the kind, although that is the correct interpretation. What I said to him was, "Joe, you don't want me to make you pregnant." That is what I mean by a transference interpretation; it is always verbally and emotionally related to the therapist. What you convey to the patient is not only the meaning of what he has done but the emotional effect his behavior has on you. It is not enough to make the patient understand the unconscious meaning of a symptom. He must know that his actions affect others and that other people care about him enough to react personally and strongly to what he does.

In other words, you cannot treat a patient unless you are prepared to participate in the psychosis. I referred to this in the second
paper when I described a young male patient who imagined himself
flying over the Atlantic Ocean in an airplane which was going
around and around. He suddenly sighted his mother floating on
the water, got her centered, and then dive-bombed her. After this
beautiful symbolic expression of incest, he screamed, "Don't cut
off my balls, Papa." With an excited catatonic patient, it is difficult to listen to all that screaming and be able to make any sense
out of it. Impulsively, I screamed back, *"All right, I won't cut off
your balls. I'm your papa and I won't cut off your balls."* In this
case I actually assumed the rôle of the father, and only by doing
so could I make the reassuring contact with him that resolved
his psychosis.

Another patient, a most disturbed boy, was with me almost
day and night and kept repeating, "You know the score, you know
what's going on. Why are they doing this to me? Let me go before
the judge and have it over with. I know I'm going to be electro-
cuted. Call the police." He was in a violent rage, but the underlying panic never let up for a moment. Day and night his super-
ego gave him no peace. It would have done no good to tell him
that his unconscious superego was accusing him of being a murderer because of his death wishes and that he felt he had to be
murdered in return. *"Very well,"* I said finally. *"If that's the case,
I'll go to court right now and finish this matter."* I kept the patient in suspense for about three days, during which time I
reported to him several times a day about bits of information I
had gleaned from people in the Police Court, Criminal Division
of Brooklyn, and speculated about the great mystery surrounding
the charges made against him. We discussed the cleverness and
treachery of the "other side" and considered the legal aid that
could be obtained for him. The patient became more and more
excited; his thoughts centered entirely around the forthcoming
trial, and he plagued me a hundred times a day for the "decision."
He developed obsessional compulsive symptoms concerning every
decision he made, no matter how trivial. He was in an agony of

uncertainty about whether he should use the ashtray on his right or the one on the left, about whether he should eat or not and if he should, what he should eat first, etc. He behaved as if he were sealing his fate with every decision and was terrified lest he make the wrong one. Everything I told him was calculated to maintain his suspense. Finally, on the third evening, when he could stand it no longer, I rushed in, very excited, shouting, *"What do you think? You'll never guess what happened in court. Judge G. wouldn't let the case go to the jury. Imagine that! All that for nothing. Do you know what you were accused of? What do you think those bastards tried to hang you for? They told their story to the judge and he became very annoyed. He said, 'Fornication is no crime in New York State. Case dismissed!' You sure got away with it. You're a free man."* The patient was visibly affected by this good news. He couldn't believe it, and I had to repeat the story to him again and again. Suddenly his face darkened, "Oh," he said, "I get it now. I have to be cut up into little pieces and fed to the tigers." The patient did not give up his expectation of talionic reprisal, he expressed his delusion in a more primitive form, centering around his early phantasies of a cannibalistic incorporation of his mother. This was substantiated by a whole night of retching and vomiting and trying to get rid of something through a bowel movement, something that was "torturing his stomach." I lost no time in calling to his attention the kind of torture that his "mother's milk" was creating in him. Concerning the dynamics of the case, I refer you to Lewin's oral triad. (See footnote, p. 150.)

Another device, which is a way of "boring from within" a patient's delusion, is what I call "the trick against the trick." In 1951, I first interviewed a paranoid patient at one of the veterans' hospitals in New York City. Ten years before, he had come to the attention of the police by way of the F.B.I. He imagined that he was wanted by the F.B.I. for burning down the shrine of Ste. Anne de Beaupré. The fact that he had been placed in a mental institution at that time instead of being arrested appeared immaterial to him. He expected the police to apprehend him at any moment and then see that he was punished for his fancied crime.

I enlisted the aid of several members of the staff and briefed them on their respective rôles. Two would be F.B.I. agents, who would pretend to have identification cards and a typewritten list which would presumably be a compilation of those criminals still at large who were wanted for arson. I was going to lead the patient on to a complete repetition of his delusional idea, and at a certain point I would interrupt and maintain that I was the one who burned down Ste. Anne de Beaupré. Another physician would immediately jump up and accuse me of being a damned liar because he had burned down Ste. Anne de Beaupré. We would see what would happen. It must be remembered that this man's superego plagued him with guilt feelings and that he felt himself to be a worthless person. This had much deeper implications, of course, but our immediate problem was to diminish his guilt feelings while giving him some awareness that his ego was trying to overcome these feelings by being great, even if it meant being notorious. In this ridiculous way, he was trying to compensate for his sense of unworthiness.

The material was elicited from the patient as usual. Nothing new was added and as soon as the patient had finished his story, I said very angrily, *"You're a damn liar. You think by your cheap trick you can get your name into the papers. You can't get away with that with me. You know damn well that I burned down Ste. Anne de Beaupré."* The patient hardly had time to hear what I said when a staff doctor jumped to his feet, shouting, "The hell with both of you guys. You can't get away with this. I burned down Ste. Anne de Beaupré." At this point the two F.B.I. agents announced that we were all under arrest on suspicion of burning down Ste. Anne de Beaupré. They had us cornered, and everybody acted frightened, including the patient. "What's your name? And your name? And your name?" they asked quickly. "Get out the list, Joe. Are these guys on the list?" He quickly ran through the typewritten sheet of presumed arson suspects, all of us waiting intently for the result. Our names were not there. The patient questioned the credentials of the F.B.I. agents, and, taking out cards which they did not show the patient, they described them accurately, according to the patient's questioning. The patient knew what such cards should be like from his former experiences with the F.B.I. and now, as we had expected, acted as though he was convinced. The agents walked out, muttering in disgust, "A bunch of cheap publicity hounds." I sat down with the patient again and remonstrated with him, "Now see what you've done. You've made fools of all of us." He was quite confused and kept repeating, "I can't figure it out. They were F.B.I. agents, all right."

It was apparent to all of us that, though shocked by this turn of events, the patient was nevertheless interested in an exciting way as he had never been interested before. I talked with him further and still pretended I was angry when I sent him back to the ward. Four days later, for the first time the patient uneasily accepted the facts that he was in a mental institution, that his ideas were crazy, and that it was not surprising that the F.B.I. agents had sent him to a hospital when he first went to them. Over the next five weeks, the delusional system evaporated completely, and in its place was a timid, frightened man, facing reality and being considered for discharge on convalescent status.* The trick against the trick serves only as an opening wedge to make possible the flow of material that offers hope of rehabilitation. It is imperative that this device be used only when continuing therapy is available. The defenses must be replaced by a total relationship to the therapist.

While what I call the trick against the trick may seem like a very aggressive exploitation of a patient's delusion, the patient is the first one to use a "trick." His delusion is a trick devised by his unconscious censorship faculties to hide from consciousness something basically more dangerous to him than the delusion itself. He is himself deluded, and in defending his psychotic reality, he deludes others, too. I want to make clear that patients are never cured by the trick against the trick, although the use of

* The patient was subsequently discharged from the hospital and has been doing well with occasional psychotherapy. The delusion has not returned.

this device sometimes helps to push them toward greater insight. There is some danger, of course, that the patient may move toward further regression. I do not worry about regressive changes, however, because I have found very often that a patient has to get sicker before he can get well. It is my belief that the unconscious portion of the ego can sometimes handle a regressive psychic conflict with greater understanding than a representation of the same conflict at a higher level of development. In the case of the patient who was concerned about the court decision, for example, I asked him, after he recovered, what had happened inside of him during the treatment. He answered, "You did not introduce reality. Nothing can do that. You introduced a bigger unreality, and then I got totally confused and went to pieces. I suspected that it was a fake." He could tell me no more than this, but I told him that in so far as he was able to apply enough judgment to suspect that it was a fake, he was testing reality where he had not been testing it before. The trick against the trick sometimes produces important therapeutic movement, either backward or forward, in cases that seem to have reached a standstill. This device gives a kind of leverage that enables the therapist to use the delusional material of the patient to draw his attention away from his interior preoccupations and act them out in a treatment situation.

Another way of confronting the patient with reality is to call his bluff dramatically in regard to some delusion and then point out the absurdity of his behavior. I did this with the patient mentioned above, who was concerned about the judge's decision, and whined endlessly that he was going to be cut up into little pieces and fed to the tigers. When I could stand no more of this, I walked into his room with a big knife, saying, *"All right, if you're so anxious to be cut up, I'll cut you up."* He acted as if I had suddenly gone crazy, backed up against the wall and prepared to defend himself very energetically. When I did nothing, he grinned sheepishly and sat down. We had a long and profitable session together afterwards.

A young girl patient had a pillow which she carried around all the time and referred to as her son Stevie. She rocked the pillow, read to it, responded to its cries. She projected all her hallucinations on that pillow. I wanted her to project onto me. At a certain point, I grabbed the pillow and banged it on the floor, saying, *"See, that can't be a baby. I threw it on the floor with all my might and it didn't cry."* She said, "That's right, the baby didn't cry." Very shortly thereafter she abandoned her pillow-baby. By reducing a patient's delusion to absurdity, the therapist is appealing to that tiny portion of the ego that is in contact with reality. A maneuver like this acts as a wedge in the patient's psychosis and very often induces the patient to renounce some of his delusions and hallucinations and project them on the therapist.

Now when you systematically attack a patient's psychosis by the technique described above, you have to be prepared sooner or later to face the aggression that will surely be mobilized. The aim of therapy is to direct this aggression toward the therapist rather than to have the patient dissipate it amorphously in his usual schizophrenic fashion. According to analytic theory, these aggressive feelings probably originate in the anal-sadistic period and are inhibited from expression by the talion principle: an eye for an eye and a tooth for a tooth; if one eats, one will be eaten.* The patient, for example, who imagines he is the Holy Trinity, instead of accepting the fact that he is a nasty guy who wants to kill everybody, defends himself against retaliation by denying his aggression and asserting the opposite: that he is God's vicar on earth, or something equally lofty, and loves and protects every-

---

* Melanie Klein was the first to point out that the later stages of earliest infancy are characterized by cannibalism. The infant nurses and the breast disappears. The child has the feeling that he has eaten it up, swallowed it, destroyed it. This is the beginning of cannibalistic ideas. Momentarily the child has a depressed, frightened feeling which I am sure has been described by many theoretic analysts as the feeling of having been eaten. Bertram Lewin, particularly, has referred to the oral triad. The infant eats; he is eaten up in turn. Then he goes to sleep. The baby comes to respect the magical power of the breast. He eats it up; it reappears. The milk keeps right on flowing, and the process takes on a magical quality. The magical reappearance of the breast makes it possible for the baby to keep on eating.

body. When the protective delusion is destroyed, the awful truth that lurks behind that loving facade threatens to emerge into consciousness. Since, to the schizophrenic mind, the wish is equivalent to the deed, the patient cannot even recognize the existence of his own death wishes. To admit the death wishes would be tantamount to perpetrating the crime and would invite retaliation just as certainly as would the actual crime itself. The analyst can now assure the patient that his death wish will be powerless against him, and when aggressive behavior is actually released, the physician can control the patient physically and prove to him in this way that the physician is stronger than the magic of the schizophrenia. He can also prove that there will be no retaliation. Sometimes, when I have the patient pinned to the floor, I say, *"I can castrate you. I can kill you, I can eat you. I can do whatever I want to you, but I am not going to do it."* The patient gets the feeling of having met a master who could do anything he wanted to him by virtue of his physical strength but will not do it because he loves him. The patient is usually relieved from anxiety, feels safe, and is much closer to reality. Sometimes, when the patient is thus immobilized, I have talked through a tremendous amount of material and gained a significant advantage for future treatment.

I should like to add a word here about the danger of suicide and homicide. If you block a patient's suicide by sheer force, he is liable to turn this aggression which has been turned inward, toward you, the therapist. You cannot be too careful in protecting patients of this type from harming themselves or others.

If you were to hear me calling a patient "crazy," for example, or shouting at him angrily, or struggling on the floor with him, you might feel that I was being too severe or perhaps even cruel to him. But this aspect of therapy in no way violates the over-riding principle of constant love and protection. The schizophrenic, like the child, I feel, can be depended upon to differentiate between the mother who gives candy occasionally as a token of love and affection and the mother who gives candy all the time so that the child will be no bother. The child understands the difference between the mother who denies love but gives candy, and the mother who gives love but may deny candy out of concern for the child's welfare, perhaps even slapping his hand when he has taken the forbidden candy. Being an indulgent parent when deprivation is indicated does no service to the patient and may undermine successful treatment.

As treatment progresses, what are the steps in recovery? Many patients whom I have treated successfully were, at the outset, completely silly and dilapidated. Others were not so deeply regressed. I have observed that they all seem to go through similar steps in recovering, starting, of course, from whatever level of regression existed at the outset of treatment. These definite steps can be marked even though many different types of symptoms may be present at any stage.

When the patient who has regressed to the very lowest level— a silly, neologistic hebephrenia which sometimes approaches a kind of catatonia, almost an intra-uterine state—begins to improve, he develops a kind of paranoia which lasts for some time. When he comes out of his paranoia, he goes into a manic-depressive phase, with either mania or depression predominating. The swing from the one to the other may be a matter of hours or only minutes. Then he develops obsessive-compulsive behavior, walking over lines again and again, shifting a spoon in and out of a plate, going through all kinds of rituals, etc. But you don't get the discouraged feeling you do when you watch an obsessional-compulsive neurotic, and usually it doesn't last long at all. Sometimes these patients are able to stop this kind of behavior on command. When this set of symptoms is given up, anxiety attacks come on with sweating, paleness, trembling, cold hands and feet. The next line of defense is psychosomatic. The patient develops hypochondriasis, complains of headaches, gastrointestinal symptoms, and very often asthma. I never saw so many cases of asthma as I have since I started treating schizophrenics. When the psychosomatic symptoms disappear, the patient begins to show mature, genital behavior. I cannot see that the kind of neurosis or psychosomatic complaints that the recovering schizophrenic suffers differ greatly from what I have observed in nonschizophrenic patients. The upward or downward course of illness suggests that we are dealing with recognizable stages of a single process, and it is, of course, of the greatest advantage to fit treatment to the current level.

Skilled use of direct analysis requires at any stage the soundest possible knowledge of the unconscious, and this means sound training. If you don't know the unconscious, you are just about as licked as you are on the golf course if you haven't got a sound swing; you may occasionally hit the ball where you want it to go but more often you will hit it into the woods. You really have to know the unconscious to know how to interpret. And the best way I know to gain knowledge of the unconscious is through a personal analysis. In the course of a personal analysis (whether you call it therapeutic or didactic is immaterial if it is successful), the portion of the ego which keeps the unconscious in check yields somewhat, and parts of the unconscious come into consciousness. Here you have an unparalleled chance to sense what the schizophrenic patient is constantly experiencing and to know what lurks in your dreams and his nightmares.

I should like to add a word in closing about prognosis. Although I have never found a patient who did not respond to direct analysis, not all patients get as well as one would like. At the outset of treatment, patients are at different levels of regression; I think of the initial level as the base line "A", in terms of which I measure improvement. Sometimes after working with a patient for a year or two, there is improvement to a higher level of maturity which I call "B". I am not certain at this time, however, that continuing to work with such a patient will bring him up from "B" to "C", a still higher level of maturity. This is true of two patients whom I continue to treat. Fortunately, most of the patients recover to a very comfortable level of maturity. I have found that it seems important for them to maintain a continuing relationship with me. They may see me every month, or every two months, or sometimes just at Christmas. They get married, have children, hold down good jobs, lose loved ones, and have all the usual difficulties of life, but they do not regress to a dereistic way of thinking.

In some cases, treatment is interrupted because of family hostility or because, as patients attain sufficient reality, I no longer have authority over them. But like so many children who reach the age of twenty-one and leave home, on more than one occasion they return.

Up to the present time, however, I am not prepared to concede the hypothetical hopeless case.

An Initial Interview

I HAVE ALWAYS FOUND the experience of the initial therapeutic interview an exciting challenge. I look upon my patient as a vast unknown containing a lifetime of influences, certain of which were so hurtful they made it impossible for him to live in the world of reality. From friends and family, we of course obtain the usual anamnestic data, but this is someone's intellectual description of the patient from his point of view, and as the years go on, I come to rely upon it less eagerly than heretofore. It is up to me to discover as quickly as possible what the real adverse forces were. For my part, I bring to this task my background of training and experience in psychoanalysis and whatever resourcefulness I have at my command. According to our concept of optimum conditions, it is hoped that the patient will bring a flow of productions which, like dream material, will both contain and disguise the noxious content below.

I have selected this as a more typical example of the kind of interviews I have. However, one must be equally prepared for an extreme divergence, as, for example, with a mute catatonic where the entire interview might consist of my finding an immediate approach to muteness based on a general understanding of the patient's fear and resistance.

I would like to spell out a few general concepts which will be useful. It is important for future treatment that in the initial interview (1) the patient realize that the therapist is on his side and will help him and fight for him if necessary against his attackers, real and imaginary; (2) the therapist show the patient generally by his sympathetic attitude and specifically through interpretations that he understands him and speaks his language, (the language of the primary process); and (3) the patient realize that he is regarded by the therapist as mentally ill, in plain language, as crazy.

It is important to keep in mind that the interview reported here took place before a large audience consisting of the professional personnel of a hospital, that my manner was more impersonal than is customary, and that I made fewer direct interpretations, restricting myself, for the most part, to eliciting information. However, it illustrates many characteristic techniques. When I wish to get the patient to express his ideas freely, which was my main purpose in this interview, I treat the psychotic material very casually, comparing it to dream material and suggesting sympathetic explanations to the patient. But when I want to make the patient realize that he is crazy, I respond to his psychotic ideas from the standpoint of common sense and show the patient his lack of judgment and the inappropriateness of his behavior. Direct interpretations are here offered tentatively to draw the patient out and are not made forcefully as would be the case during intensive therapy.

Interview

Dr. Rosen: *Hello Mr. J.* I am glad to have an opportunity to sit and talk with you a little bit. I am a psychiatrist practicing in New York, and I came up here to talk to these doctors and nurses and professional staff, and I was hoping that you would talk with me.*

Patient: I would be glad to talk with you, but I am afraid when I talk with you, because it's not me, it is not my mind, it is somebody else's mind.

R: *Do you have any idea of whose mind it is?*

* Patient is a 34 year old single, white male. His father died when he was 7 years of age. His mother, about 60, is living and suffers from diabetes. He is the third of seven siblings, four brothers and two sisters. Patient began to show symptoms while in service in 1944. Despite his emotional difficulties, he almost completed successfully a four year law course. During the period of his final examinations in 1950, he became acutely psychotic and had to be hospitalized.

P: Oh yes, oh yes, somebody talking to me when I sleep. Not recently but some time back. [At this point, the patient's eyes darted all over the room and the rapidity of movements and his stiffening attitude indicated that he was going through an immediate reaction.]

R: *Don't be nervous . . . . .**

P: I am nervous. This is the first time I have been sitting in front of any crowd here at all. I had so many snow jobs lately that I am afraid that this is another snow job also.

R: *No, I can assure you that . . . . .*

P: I am sitting here and talking to them because I am, I am anxious to get the hell out of here.

R: *But what you just said to me before about this mind talks to you when you are asleep and something happening a long time ago. Is it possible that this is the mind that used to talk to you when you used to dream before you got sick?*

P: Absolutely impossible. What I mean, I don't know how far it goes back, it goes back, I don't know, in the last two years, two and a half years.

R: *You have been hearing this mind for the last two and a half years?*

P: I haven't been hearing this mind, but I have been thinking this mind.

R: *It's very interesting that you put it that way for this reason, every human being has two minds. One mind they are not very familiar with and, it's called the unconscious mind; did you ever hear of that when you were in law school? . . . . . The unconscious mind which governs the dreams and fantasy thoughts, and interferes with you when you want to remember somebody's name, and it won't let you, and when you begin to feel that mind, it actually seems like a stranger is intruding on your mind; you're not used to it.*

P: Look at it this way. In my family, reported family, it is brown

* Series of dots indicate pause or interruption.

eyes, that's where I grew up, it was a hard life, there were a lot of tears, a lot of misery, a lot of knocks, some happences *—brown eyes, brown eyes, brown eyes, brown eyes. Years later in Boston, three or four years later, even before then my companions, back in '45 or so, I can't go back over all my life.

R: *No, it's not necessary.*

P: There was a blue-eyed friend here and a blue-eyed friend there and a blue-eyed friend there. A masculine friend . . . . .

R: *Blue-eyed friends were always masculine?*

P: Oh no, I say in this particular instance.

R: *I see.*

P: Leading up to the present developments, leading up to the so-called Freudian father, the love of the penis, etc.

R: *Where did you hear about that stuff?*

P: I don't know where I heard it. My mind probably told me.

R: *This other mind told you these things. . . . . . So?*

P: So after the war, I'm in Maine, there was uncertainty in my life. What is this life? Is it a real life or is it just phony? If I say this isn't my family, this isn't my mother, this isn't my father, this isn't my brother, these aren't my friends here, that isn't my school, this isn't my life. Everything comes out, what you call a mental or psychic suicide, not a physical suicide, but a psychic suicide. Everything comes out. So I got afraid. [Seemingly bizarre but nevertheless true; the destruction of one's reality is suicide.]

R: *Ummm . . . . . May I interrupt you?*

P: Sure.

R: *Get your real mind listening to me now. I wonder whether this thing that came up wasn't this sort of dream mind that you began to feel while you were awake.*

P: You mean when I felt the unreality of my . . . . .

*As stated (neologism).

R: *Yes. Because all this crazy stuff about this eyes, that eyes*
. . . . .

P: I went out on a tangent. Wait a minute. I left the eyes for a moment.

R: *Yes.*

P: We'll come back to the eyes. This was back in '46, say '47
. . . . .

R: *Did you ever see anything of those modernistic or bizarre paintings with all kinds of eyes staring around at people?*

P: Not especially. . . . . . No.

R: *Have you ever seen any of that work at all?* . . . . . *The eyes are a very important part of the unconscious.*

P: Yes sir. So the eyes in the family is brown eyes. As I said I felt this uncertainty after the war, the more I felt the uncertainty, the more I told myself that it wasn't so. I kicked the uncertainty out. So we're in Boston and life remains pretty tough. It becomes more insecure all the time. So I meet a young lady, she has blue eyes, she has my mannerisms and my own expressions, at the same time, before or while I met her someone was plotting to me in my sleep.

R: *Was that a dream?*

P: Oh no, this was fact . . . . . and she was saying the same things that were being said to me in my unconscious mind or some of the things anyway.

This material means that the patient's incorporated superego is the mother. Once incorporated, it is also himself. The unconscious cannot distinguish between the mother and self. (In the beginning mouth and breast were one and in the unconscious they remain one.) It may perhaps be valid to say that the eyes in their taking-in process in the earliest infancy feel like the mouth. However, an interpretation to this effect can only be valuable therapeutically to a psychotic. The same interpretation may become valuable to a neurotic after many years of analysis when the diminished resistances allow the unconscious to come close enough to conscious vision so that knowledge of the existence of mother and self as one can promote affect.

R: *Uh huh.*

P: And she had some of my mannerisms too.

R: *Who do you take after in your family?*

P: I hope to God nobody.

R: *But whom do you look like? Do you look like your father or your mother?*

P: I don't know, it's a pretty sorry state, isn't it.

R: *No, I don't know, maybe you just don't want to tell me, or you have a feeling that you take after your father or mother or sister or brother or somebody but you don't want to tell me for some reason or other.*

P: Take after my father or mother . . . . . but they weren't my father nor my mother.

R: *In other words, your parents weren't really your parents.*

P: No, no, they aren't.

R: *All right, that's a good thing . . . . . in some ways. Do you know who your father or mother are?*

P: No, I don't.

R: *You have no idea? . . . . . But you don't feel you belong to your father or mother?*

P: No . . . . . No . . . . . Not to them I don't.

R: *It is very confusing.*

P: It isn't so confusing as it's agonizing.

R: *In fact, I'd say it is agonizing. I don't know who you belong to, maybe they treated you in such a way that you felt you didn't belong to them, and that feeling stayed in your unconscious mind all the time. And now it comes back to plague you by saying you don't belong, you don't belong. They can't be your parents the way they treat you.*

P: I am not worried whether they belong to me, my family or not. I'm just worried about what's been happening so that I know where I stand, where and how.

R: *Well, the way you are now you of course realize that you are crazy.*

P: No sir, I am not crazy.

R: *Well, what are you?*

P: My emotions are all gone.

R: *Well, doesn't something tell you inside of you that you are screwy?*

P: Yes, that's true, that's quite true, that's different. I know that. I know I'm in a turmoil, my emotions are gone, I said my mind isn't my own. My emotions are all gone anyway. Thinking like a woman, talking like a woman. [To make a homosexual interpretation at this time would be a serious error.]

R: *You said this woman had your characteristics.*

P: Some of them . . . . . Yeah.

R: *Well that means you had some of her characteristics.*

P: No, no, no, she was schooled, she was altogether trained, the right words, the right inflection, the right everything, everything right down to perfection. In fact her hair was like a picture of myself, of me when I was 2 or 3 years old. Picture of myself and my godfather . . . . . that was the dirtiest trick they pulled on me see.

R: *Who did?*

P: I don't know who did, that's what I want to find out. A picture of my godfather and his daughter and supposedly myself, so they told me, and I had my hair long, about two years old. And if there was any unhappiness in my family, I would probably think to myself, there, somebody looked after me.

R: *Your godfather?*

P: Not the godfather, just somebody who took care of me there.

R: *The mother who took care of you at that time.*

P: Yeah.

R: *The one who is supposed to be your own mother who you think is not?*

P: Yes, it's all a dirty trick, a dirty trick, a trick. I was a fool to bite for it at all.

R: *Listen . . . . . What were you going to bite when you were a baby?*

P: I am 34 years old.

R: *You were a baby and you had to bite something.*

P: That's true.

R: *Kind of poisoned you, didn't it?*

P: At present it seems that even though I was young, even then I was insecure in the family, so I thought that it wasn't my mother but just a brown-eyed complex. I thought I didn't belong there. This reported father died when I was 6 or 5 years old and things were so artificial at the funeral that I thought perhaps it was my father. And all the time people kept talking about my father, my father, and I kept looking at that picture. I kept building up in my mind the idea of a father. I hated my mother, but I felt sorry for her. So this time I thought I was subconsciously in love with the father and kept thinking about a father and the father's penis and something like that the way the Freudians put it. So subconsciously it was this love for the fatherly penis that when I met this blue-eyed vixen it enabled me to be completely by empathy, be myself in herself, her in me, she appeared sexual gratification, psychosexual gratification, by the father's penis, is that how you put it?

R: *Be damned if I know what you're talking about.*

P: You know damned well what I'm talking about.

R: *Sounds awfully crazy to me. But I don't know . . . . . I suppose there are some men who are homosexuals, I don't think you are, are you?*

P: Not that I know of, I don't know, I don't think so . . . . . could be, could be.

R: *If you were homosexual, you would know about it, wouldn't you?*

P: I suppose I would.

R: *You would be a fairy, hang around with fairies . . . . . well, are you?*

P: No, I didn't have any experience like that.

R: *Well what's the use of bringing that up about loving the penis?*

P: I didn't say conscious penis, I said subconscious penis.

R: *Well, what's that? . . . . . I think you've got something there.*

P: Have I?

R: *I think more in unconscious or subconscious, as you put it, the penis equals the breast, what you may have been in love with, could have been what?*

P: Could have been the subconscious penis. At the same time I was receiving a lot of banging around.

R: *Wait a second. You said you were not in love with the penis in the conscious sense?*

P: No, I don't wish it to be, I hope not.

R: *Get it straight . . . . . I am glad that you are feeling better, not so nervous any more.*

P: Seems to be a humorous topic.

R: *Is there something funny about a penis, I don't know. Strikes you funny?*

P: It's not funny, it's tragic.

R: *It doesn't seem tragic right now. If you're laughing about something tragic, it's inappropriate, isn't it? I said this conscious penis that you said no is a subconscious penis. In the subconscious the penis equals the breast.*

P: It was a mistake.

R: *Now you say you love the subconscious penis. I think you mean you love the subconscious breast, but you are afraid, more afraid than of the penis . . . . . they made you bite that stuff*

*whatever it was, and you said you hated your mother, there must
have been a reason why. . . . . . Did you say here tonight that
you hated her? . . . . . I am not trying to trick you I
know that you are a lawyer, and you could probably trick me.*

P: I said I wished to hell I had killed the bitch now. [By the
time he was 4 years old, he had lived through the birth of four
siblings with the loss of the already lost mother being repeated.]

R: *Well can you think of any reason why you hated her so?*

P: Yes, she showed me her ass once.

R: *Did you look at it?*

P: Yes, she asked me if she had a pimple on it.

R: *What did you do?*

P: I just stood up. She said "Is there a pimple on my ass?" I
was 4 years old, I looked at it and told her there wasn't.

R: *And you remembered that to this day? Is that really something you remembered, or is that a crazy idea?*

P: That's fact.

R: *You got me mixed up. I don't trust lawyers.*

P: You got me mixed up.

R: *You're the lawyer. . . . . . Wait a second. Let me get myself
straightened out, will you Bud? You told me before that you
didn't have a mother and father in the usual way and then you tell
me your mother had you look at a pimple on her ass. You've got
me mixed up, you see? . . . . . What's the story? Have you got
a mother and you lost your father when you were five, is that it?*

P: As I said before, you don't remember who your mother or
father are, you don't care when you were born.

R: *That's right.*

P: I live with these people, I thought . . . . .

R: *Is this the woman you thought was your mother? What the
hell is this pay-off, is she your mother or isn't she?*

P: I don't remember being in her uterus.

R: *Well listen . . . . . Is that the criterion which makes any-*

body say this is my mother, or do you take a look at your birth certificate, if you've got any sense? If you're in doubt?

P: That's no good either.

R: *Or did they phony up about this a bit? Do you still feel strongly that she was not your mother?*

P: Not strongly, I know.

R: *You agree when you were born you weren't watching it. Let me ask you something else. After you were born, were there any brothers or sisters born?*

P: Two girls and two boys.

R: *After you? How old were you when the next kid came? It must have been a lot because your father died when you were 5. She must have had a kid every year. . . . . . Why that pimple on her ass disturbs you so has got me going.*

P: It's not disturbing, I just happened to think of it.

R: *Did looking at her ass excite you . . . . . indecently?*

P: No, no, it didn't. I just happened to think of it. I have been doing a lot of thinking lately about the past.

R: *You know what made me ask about possible brothers and sisters, you describe that mountain of adipose tissue. It was a horrible sight because you knew you would be losing her to those other kids. One after another. That's terrific. That's a great psychic blow.*

P: That was after.

R: *Maybe you thought she was going to have another, by that time you were furious. You can understand that—you went to college; you were a year old and you lose your mother to some new snip that comes along. Did the other kids feel that she is not their mother too?*

Again the patient's eyes began to dart around the room, and his rapid movements and stiffening attitude indicated that he was going through an immediate reaction.

P: Well the youngest were twins and they were taken to what you call a Social Center home, like an orphanage, and they were there until they were 3 or 4 years old.

R: *Were they really her kids? Were you there when they were born?*

P: Yes. I know when they were born.

R: *In the House?*

P: Yes.

R: *That's a hell of a thing to subject a little kid to.*

P: Everyone is subjected to that, aren't they?

R: *Ordinarily a kid of 5 years old or 4, they are not standing around or near when the mother is having a baby, that's quite something for a kid to handle. I guess your mother wasn't too smart in the way she brought you up and maybe the way she treated you, maybe you had good reason not to believe she was your mother. After all, the mother is supposed to love a kid and be devoted to the kid.*

P: I was always devoted to her and tried to help along in the poverty of the family.

R: *There must be something there, I can't quite see it yet. I am sure that if I spent a lot of time talking this thing over with you . . . . .*

P: How about the goose when I was swimming at R———, the guy gave me a goose and it made me think he was trying to shove a penis up my ass.

R: *That's a great sport.*

P: How is it different people kept telling me about it?

R: *You might have had the crazy thought that you might have wanted to try that, see?*

P: No, no.

R: *If you have had the crazy thought that you were a girl or exchanging with a girl . . . . . You have to admit that you have plenty of crazy thoughts. Look! Isn't it quite common for one guy to goose another?*

P: I am not talking about the goosing experience in itself, that's different altogether.

R: *A goose is a representation of someone sticking a prick up your ass . . . . .*

P: That's true, but the idea . . . . .

R: *Or an enema or something.*

P: Well the incident happened when I was 9 or 10 years old. Then I worked for this shoemaker and I hated working in that cobbler shop. To me he was absolute dirt.

R: *In what way?*

P: Who the hell wants to work?

R: *This is real? Not part of the insanity?*

P: This is real, the past . . . . ., so I hated the guy because I hated being confined in there. He never spoke to me and I never spoke to him except for work.

R: *Except in connection with the job.*

P: Occasionally something else. This was for six years. He used to look at me funny with his eyes, his brown eyes. He accused me once. He said, "what happened to you at the swimming hole anyway? I heard something happened to you." Then he gave me a sort of derisive look with his brown eyes. Well I hated the guy, I always did, and I was all locked up in myself, in my own work, my own school studies. And I became sort of sensitive to his look and everytime he looked like that it would sort of throw me back. And then a few other people not making direct remarks, but indirect remarks, so I became ass conscious.

R: *Naturally when your mother made you look at her ass, that's all the looking that went on there—it's a funny thing, isn't it?*

P: When do I get out of here? In as much as I have been such a service to you psychiatrists, don't you think I ought to get a better break than this, a better life?

R: *Why the hell don't you get well instead of being such a dope?*

P: How am I such a dope?

R: *I don't know . . . . . going around talking about eyes all the time. Try and understand it. Dr. Vecchione was trying to show some of these things to you, I am sure, I don't know what to say about that. How can you go out—talking all this nonsense and crazy talk. How do you think you would do out of here?*

P: You want me to just sit and have everything get out of your life, conscious and subconscious?

R: *You can't get everything out. You should be able to figure out yourself this excitement about eyes had something to do with your mother making you look at her ass. And as might have been, I wouldn't be a bit surprised that you yourself were curious and took a look at her. You wouldn't remember that, and maybe looking at her, maybe that's the way you thought she had intercourse. If you could think you were the blue-eyed girl, the waitress, and you think you were the mother and your father would fuck you and then you would get these crazy Freudian ideas.*

P: Dr. V. told me that.

R: *He told you that . . . . . you just have to put your mind to this thing and try to understand it. Talk it over with your Doctor, make him try to understand it better than anyone else. Your preoccupation with eyes is something you know about that no one else knows. Something in you that's making you do it. In order to get to understand the meaning of all this crazy talk and . . . . .*

P: What I want to know is `. . . . .` I'm locked up on that ward, I'm locked up for a long time now. I come here for a conference or whatever you want to call it. Instead of keeping quiet and listening to you talk and telling me to get well and get the hell out of here fast, I have an impulse to speak simply because I am here in front of a lot of people, what the hell is wrong with that?

R: *Nothing . . . . . Maybe you're me . . . . . I have an impulse to speak too in front of all these people. One thing about insanity is that you can identify yourself with other people. You've heard of crazy people who say "I'm Jesus Christ." That means they want to be Jesus Christ. They think they are. The unconscious*

*can do that—listen to me—can fool you into thinking that you're
your mother.*

P: What do you have to tell me to get out of here, to get well?

R: *How do you feel now?*

P: Just because I sit down here and talked with still the unconscious desire for the infantile penis. If that's what it is.

R: *I don't know what you mean by that. What's the infantile
penis, is that a pimple?*

P: This isn't a joke. [Here patient speaks hurriedly with more
volume, and with a considerable amount of hostility.] Alright
. . . . . I'm afraid. I'm a coward, but that doesn't mean you can
stand there and make a GD fool out of me. You know what I
want to do. You know what's the matter with me. You know
damn well what's the matter with me because you made me that
way, you've got me cooped up in there. I want to get out of there.
You just frustrate my emotions. I just want to leave the place,
that's all, that's the matter with me. I'm too much of a God damned
fool to speak up, that's all, that's the matter with me.

R: *Now you feel angry.*

P: I don't feel angry.

R: *You sound angry. It's all right to be angry, if I were cooped
up there I would get angry too. That's a healthy emotion.*

P: It's all my fault.

R: *Why do you say it's your fault, what did you do wrong?*

P: For being a GD fool and expecting any possibility, any hope
of getting out of here, by coming in and talking to you people.

R: *Did anybody promise you that if you came here and talked to
me you would get out of this place?*

P: Nobody did. But I thought perhaps it might.

R: *I don't consider you cured because I talked to you for 40
minutes or a half hour or so.*

P: You're crazier than I am.

R: *Possibly . . . . . What's the matter, does your leg hurt?*

P: Yeah, it's asleep. . . . . . What's the upshot of this whole thing?

R: *I don't know how much you understand.*

P: I know what you understand. You get a joker, I'm upstairs. I feel suppressed, I feel rotten, so you bring me down here in front of all these people. My ego goes off. My fake mind starts to talk—uteruses, infantile paralysis, and all that shit, all that . . . . . what happens, I leave here, I'm confused, more and more confused. I am more confused, more and more suppression upstairs, I'm locked up, my mind goes off again.

R: *What does that mean?*

P: Confusion—just plain confusion.

R: *Well, if the unconscious mind is working when it is supposed to be buried out of sight it's bound to be confusing. That is what insanity is, the unconscious mind intruding on . . . . .*

P: Don't explain. All I want to do is get well and get the hell out of here. So will explaining psychiatry help me any?

R: *Yes, I think it will. I think if you understood all of these things that are bothering you, you would be well.*

P: I don't think so. Suppose we start on a tangible rôle first.

R: *Go ahead, I'm trying.*

P: Answer my question, you can't help me that way, so . . . . . more and more confusion to come here, sit around and talk, pretty blond here, Dr. V. looking at me with a fatherly interest, a couple of psychiatrists over there. My ego goes up again. I go upstairs.

[Long sigh by the patient.]

R: *What you say is true. If you give up some of these notions you will get very confused and very disturbed. You are probably beginning to get sense, the realization that you are a sick man. Just being out of here wouldn't cure you.*

P: Well, may I make a suggestion?

R. *Please do.*

P: You psychiatrists have had me now for a couple of years, other hospitals and here, suppose you take me out of that ward where I am now and place me in another ward.

R: *Would that help you?*

P: Oh yes, it would help me, I mean in a better ward where I would have the freedom of the grounds around here, and I can go and come as I please. You know I would get cured in no time at all.

R: *I doubt it. I bet you doubt it too.*

P: I would feel much better, I know that.

R: *Yes, you would get promoted to another ward. It would be good for your ego, and possibly make you feel that you were getting better.*

P: Are these people all psychiatrists here?

R: *They are all part of the professional personnel here, connected with this hospital. I don't know if they are all psychiatrists. I don't know them all either. I come from New York.*

P: What do you have to tell me that I can understand? Not in psychiatric terms. Something in my lay mind I can understand, that will give me an idea, if you want to, some definite hope of how long before I can . . . . .

R: *Before you can what?*

P: Leave. I don't want to sit here and argue with you and tell you that I know your business. I don't. I know I don't. I just want to tell you what is on my mind, that's all. What is your program here anyway? Can you give me a definite idea, am I leaving here sometime?

R: *What do you think about it?*

P: I don't know, no idea.

R: *How do you feel right now? Is that other mind talking to you or are you a whole person at this moment.*

P: I'm telling you in my heart how I feel, I want to get out of here.

R: *I feel that too, but you haven't answered my question. What is talking now, a whole you, or that other mind?*

P: My feelings are talking, my unhappiness is talking.

R: *Is that you or that unconscious mind?*

P: It is me.

R: *Do you understand what I told you about how the unconscious mind intrudes on you like a vicious stranger? Do you understand that? . . . . . You don't get that at all, it still seems like somebody else.*

P: On the other hand, suppose while looking at these eyes at home, and I do not love those eyes.

R: *Whose eyes are they?*

P: My mother's eyes, say, we'll say she wasn't really my mother, let's assume that. So I look at those eyes and there's no love there. But wanting love I can only go back to when I was 1 or 2 years old.

R: *Yes.*

P: So the only love I had was when I was 1 or 2 years old, genuine love, so if you empty my life out, and empty my love out . . . . . what the hell is there left to my mind?

R: *There's just one hitch. If you went back to 1 year old, you would find less love than you feel right now. I don't think your mother loved you. It's your hope that by regressing and regressing to your earliest infancy you will find what you never had and couldn't get from your mother.*

P: I have been afraid of being psychically empty here. I have been afraid of emptying my mind psychically and someone would knock me on the head and give me amnesia and there wouldn't be anything left at all.

R: *Oblivion? That won't happen. I know too much about your kind of case. You won't find oblivion, that's not the way out . . . . . The only hope of your recovery is for you to gain a real understanding of this whole mess.*

P: Help me get an understanding then.

R: *I wish I were up here, I would.*

P: Well, how do I get an understanding?

R: *There are other doctors here, perfectly well qualified to help you.*

P: How am I getting better just sitting in the ward walking back and forth, having everybody gesticulating, sticking a penis up my ass?

R: *I notice from your record here that quite a bit of effort is being expended on helping you understand things, and you have to distinguish between a penis actually being shoved up your ass and your imagination that this is happening.*

P: Yes, I see that. Good night! If you sit in a place locked up, locked up, locked up, and don't know what's going on. Do you think . . . . . I can distinguish the difference, but at the same time you say to yourself, what the hell is going on, you say to yourself what the hell is going on? It's disgusting.

R: *When the unconscious mind intrudes on you that way it is disgusting, and what is more it makes you mad. And if I can't stop it one, two, three, you get mad at me.*

P: You're not helping me any now. You're just confusing me.

R: *All right, you go back to your ward. So long kid.*

Some Observations on Bleuler's Conception of Dementia Praecox

EUGEN BLEULER'S *Dementia Praecox or the Group of Schizophrenias,** was originally published in German in 1911. It seems incredible that this work which revolutionized psychiatric thinking should have been denied to English speaking psychiatrists for more than 40 years. We are indebted to all who had a hand in its publication, especially to Dr. Joseph Zinkin, the translator.

Bleuler, a sensitive and painstaking student, began his investigations in the 1880's when psychiatric research was limited mainly to brain pathology and diagnostic criteria were only in the process of formulation. In 1899, Kraepelin classified the so-called "deteriorating psychoses" under the heading of Dementia Praecox, subdividing this group according to its predominant catatonic, hebephrenic, or paranoid symptomatology. These diagnoses were based on what Bleuler came later to call accessory symptoms— delusions, hallucinations, motor expressions, silly behavior, etc. Many patients who showed these symptoms suffered from alcoholism, infectious diseases, senility, or other organic involvements that had only an incidental connection with the functional psychoses but were grouped with them because of the apparent similarity of symptomatology. Bleuler's great contribution was the discovery that only in true dementia praecox were what he called the fundamental symptoms to be found: disturbances of association and affectivity, intense ambivalence, and a predilection for fantasy as against reality. He also pointed out that in certain cases

---

* Translated by Joseph Zinkin, M.D. New York, International Universities Press, 1950, 548 pp.

of alcoholism, where the accessory symptoms were usually attributed to the alcohol consumed, the fundamental symptoms were also present. In these cases, he felt that the alcoholism itself could be understood as a secondary manifestation of the fundamental (schizoid) process. This was equally true for other predominantly organic syndromes where the underlying fundamental symptoms could be found. By isolating for the first time the specific symptomatology of the dementia praecox group of psychoses, Bleuler went to a considerable distance toward bringing order out of the well-nigh hopeless confusion existing at that time. In place of the misleading term "dementia praecox," which had become meaningless since these patients showed neither the dementia nor the precocious onset formerly associated with the disease, Bleuler coined the word, "schizophrenia"—to emphasize the fundamental disharmony or "split" in the personality that was specific for this disorder and for no other.

Although Bleuler understood and never lost interest in the possible organic origin of schizophrenia (as evidenced, for example, by the fact that he uses the term deterioration sometimes in an organic and sometimes in a non-organic sense), he directed his attention mainly toward the psychology of schizophrenia. To further his understanding of this disease, he did something which very few psychiatrists have ever done. For 12 years, roughly from 1885 to 1897, unhampered by family ties or outside interests, he devoted himself to a study of the schizophrenic patients at the mental hospital in Rheinau, Switzerland. He lived at the hospital and spent almost all his time with patients, lending them a sympathetic ear and bending every effort to understand what they were saying and doing. He left Rheinau to become the Director of Burghölzli, with Jung as his first assistant. During the next decade, he made an intensive study of Freud's works, became acquainted with Freud personally, and worked in close collaboration with many gifted psychoanalytic minds. Bleuler's great knowledge of schizophrenia gained through his experience at Rheinau and Burghölzli, plus the insights gained through his study of psychoanalysis, made it possible for him to create a new school of dynamic psychiatry. Burghölzli became a mecca, attracting students from all over the world. Our debt to this small group of men who had such a tremendous influence on the development of dynamic psychiatry is incalculable. Our special debt to one man in particular is acknowledged by Bleuler on page 389 of his text where he says, "we still owe it only to Freud that it has become possible to explain the special symptomatology of schizophrenia."

To the modern psychiatrist who works actively with schizophrenic patients, the book will prove disappointing in some respects. Because Bleuler's influence on modern psychiatry has been so great, much of what appeared new and inspiring in 1911 is now commonplace. Bleuler's brilliant reclassification of diagnostic categories, his refinement of terminology, and his dynamic approach to mental disease have become part of our psychiatric curriculum. In a sense, then, this book is dated because it has already done the job it was intended to do. Nowadays, those of us who favor a dynamic approach take much for granted that Bleuler is at pains to explain. What the present-day psychotherapist looks for, and what is conspicuously lacking in this book, is Bleuler's method of psychotherapy. It is a reflection on the times rather than on the author that in 500 pages of text only 18 are devoted to therapy. From Bleuler's son, at present Professor of Psychiatry at the University of Zurich and Director of Burghölzli, as well as from Dr. H. Nunberg, Dr. A. A. Brill, and others, I understand that Bleuler did much psychotherapy on an experimental basis. It is unfortunate that he tells us nothing of his therapeutic approach and results.

This book, nonetheless, should be required reading for any psychiatrist who would understand and treat schizophrenic patients. As a stimulus to dynamic thinking, the case material and theoretic discussion are incomparable. The very concept of the fundamental symptoms compels the reader to think: Are they evidence of an organic predisposition as Bleuler believed or are they not rather the unrepressed manifestations of the unconscious that exists in all of us? Isn't it true that these fundamental symptoms are also found in normal people? Is there any individual free from ambivalence, disturbed affectivity and association, and a predisposition to fantasy? In the schizophrenic, to be sure, the unconscious is not controlled by the healthy resistances of the normal person and bursts forth in delusions, hallucinations, etc. Is not this difference between the normal and the schizophrenic one of degree rather than of kind? It is my belief that anyone can become schizophrenic, no matter how healthy his developmental years might have been. There is no such thing as mental health that can withstand all destructive environmental influences. I realize, of course, that there are degrees of susceptibility and that to a given trauma, one individual might respond with schizophrenic and another with neurotic symptoms. To think, however, that nothing could break the neurotic down into a schizophrenic seems to me wishful thinking. Once the shaky neurotic defenses give way, the unconscious pours out, or, in the terminology of Bleuler, both fundamental and accessory symptoms are manifested. The disappearance of the accessory symptoms and the diminished intensity of the fundamental symptoms indicate that the unconscious has been returned to where it belongs, betraying its presence only in times of stress and in dream life. But this does not mean, as Bleuler indicates, that the patient is still schizophrenic. It implies, rather, that he is potentially schizophrenic— as are we all. What constitutes cure, recovery, or even improvement, for that matter, is still debatable.

The book is replete with numerous examples of schizophrenic productions which challenge the analytic imagination of the reader and would furnish fascinating material for seminar discussion. For example, the following:

In a certain case of abortive ecstasy, the patient, after taking communion, felt, "bathed for two whole days in an infinite, heavenly happiness so that all he could do was cry with sheer joy." The schizophrenic ecstatic mood can also be transferred to quite insignificant things. Thus a catatonic with ecstatic expression verbigerates, "I have knitted, I have knitted, I have knitted, yes, indeed, I have knitted (she had never as yet done any work in the hospital); it was beautiful, wonderful! These beautiful embroidered curtains! (there were no curtains at all). When the curtains were parted, how they did sing! ("Who was there?") Mother was there, everyone was there, etc., etc. I follow the Lord God!"

Interpreted on the oral level, following B. D. Lewin's analysis of the dream screen, the embroidered curtains might represent mother's undergarment, and, when the patient says, "Mother was there," she refers to the breast, i.e., to the dream screen. The ecstasy experienced by the patient is the blissful oral satisfaction of the infant. Now following Abraham's analysis in his paper on the first, pregenital level, emphasis would be placed on the knitting (masturbation); parted curtains would be interpreted as the parted labia and the exposed genital, which the unconscious equates with the breast, provides the medium through which the patient can relive the oral ecstasy she once knew and longs to re-experience. In both instances, there is a complete merging of the ego with the superego (the mother with the child).

I ask the reader's indulgence for my personal speculations on those parts of the book most interesting to me. Bleuler's case material is unusually rich in content and lends itself readily to dynamic understanding. I found this part of the book most stimulating and, in the long run, it may prove to be the book's greatest usefulness to the modern student.

Note to Paper 9

The wide acceptance and usefulness of Bleuler's classification of schizophrenia make me hesitate to add this note, for fear of muddying rather than refining his contribution, that of assisting us forward from the Kraepelinian hodgepodge of dementia praecox. In writing the papers contained in this volume, it became increasingly difficult for me to use the term schizophrenia when what I had in mind was psychosis. When I saw enough patients who had been diagnosed manic-depressive psychosis and were now schizophrenic, I began to realize that psychotics do not differ in kind but only in degree. I became more sure of my ground when, in the course of recovery from schizophrenia, they again became manic-depressive and went on from there to neurosis. I cannot reconcile the idea of different kinds of psychosis with

Freud's concept of the unconscious. Until someone is born without an unconscious, I have to assume that everybody has one. Depending upon the amount of unconscious prevailing for any given period of time, we recognize manifest psychosis. The classification which offers the greatest hope of clarification will be one that has judgment as its yardstick. The total unconscious has absolutely no judgment. It is black. The yardstick shades through gray to the hypothetic white, which is good normal judgment with no unconscious evident. A quantitative psychologic test, using judgment as its base and having for its purpose the discovery of what per cent of the unconscious has inundated consciousness and robbed it of maturity, will give us the only clear means of applying names to the stages of mental sickness. These names will represent not different diseases, but different degrees of the same sickness. The term "psychosis" is used instead of schizophrenia in the first paper which is actually, in point of time, our latest. It is used to express our emphasis on the sameness of the whole pathologic process. This sameness, for the purposes of this paper, was more important to us than the fine shadings of diagnosis which may set up the thought that something different is involved in hebephrenia, catatonia, and paranoia, when what is involved is merely a succession of stations on the journey up or down.

Index